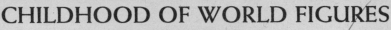

# CHILDHOOD OF WORLD FIGURES

# GANDHI

## YOUNG NATION BUILDER

by Kathleen Kudlinski

Aladdin Paperbacks
New York London Toronto Sydney

◆ ALADDIN PAPERBACKS
An imprint of Simon & Schuster Children's Publishing Division
1230 Avenue of the Americas, New York, NY 10020
Text copyright © 2006 by Kathleen Kudlinski
Cover illustrations copyright © 2006 by Todd Leonardo
All rights reserved, including the right of reproduction in whole or in part in any form.
ALADDIN PAPERBACKS and colophon are trademarks of Simon & Schuster, Inc.
CHILDHOOD OF WORLD FIGURES is a registered trademark of Simon & Schuster, Inc.
Designed by Lisa Vega
The text of this book was set in Aldine 721.
Manufactured in the United States of America
First Aladdin Paperbacks edition October 2006
10  9  8  7  6  5  4  3  2  1
Library of Congress Control Number 2006927850
ISBN-13: 978-1-4169-1283-5
ISBN-10: 1-4169-1283-5

# CONTENTS

# CHAPTER 1
# SACRED COWS, SACRED SNAKES

"Ba," Mohandas Gandhi asked his mother, "may I come to the market with you?"

"Don't you want to play with your big brothers instead?" Putlibai Gandhi asked.

Mohan pictured the neighborhood bullies. "Big ears!" they teased him in the streets. "Midget!" "Baby!" He shuddered. Mohan knew that his ears stood out. He knew he was small compared with other-six-year-olds. And he was the youngest child in the family. But his father was the dewan, the prime minister of Porbandar, India! That should count for something, Mohan thought. He stood taller.

"Very well." Putlibai pulled a length of her

sari over her smoothly combed hair. "Quiet as you are, you'll be no trouble. The driver is waiting."

Mohan and Ba stepped into the blinding sunshine in the courtyard. The barefoot driver bowed to Putlibai and then to Mohan and stepped between the rickshaw's two long handles. The Gandhis squeezed in together on the rickshaw seat. Then they leaned back as the driver picked up his handles. As he pulled them through the high gate of the family compound, the noise and confusion of the town filled Mohan's senses.

He sat tall, breathing in the tropical scent blowing off the Arabian Sea nearby and the rich smells of spicy cooking and rotting garbage from the street. Men and women thronged the dusty road, their great shirts and flowing saris a shifting rainbow of color; their chatter a mix of Bengali and Hindi languages. Other rich people in rickshaws whisked past, weaving between the people. Soon the Gandhi family driver was sprinting too. Mohan twisted in his seat to stare as a rickshaw passed carrying an English man. He sat stiff in his strange jacket and top hat.

Suddenly the rickshaw stopped. Mohan tumbled out of his seat onto the road. He stared up at the old cow that had tottered in front of them. She froze in place while traffic swerved around her. "Sorry, so sorry!" the driver was saying to the cow, and, "Sorry, Mrs. Gandhi."

"Take your time, dear old one," Putlibai called to the cow. "The Lord Vishnu is with you." The animal turned bleary eyes in Mrs. Gandhi's direction.

Mohan rubbed a scraped elbow. "Ba, you care more about the cow than you do about me!"

Patina's lips pressed together. "I revere all living things." She pointed to the cow. "You help her," she said, "for dear Vishnu." Mohan looked at his mother for a moment, then at the cow. Her bony shoulder stood higher than his head, and flies swarmed around her eyes. "Help her off the road." Mrs. Gandhi prompted.

Mohan took a breath and waved the flies from the old cow's face. Big as she was, the cow flinched. "Easy, old girl," Mohan said. He did not know how to move a cow. He picked up a twig to swat her.

"Think *ahisma*, Mohan," Ba scolded. "The ancient Hindu teaching. *Ahisma:* Nonviolence in all things."

A holy man wrapped in a yellow-gold cloak picked his way across the street and stood on the other side of the cow. "Put your hands on her," he suggested. He rested one hand on the cow's hip and another on her head. "Feel what it is like to be this cow."

Mohan tentatively patted the cow's shoulder. It was hot and firm, the fur smooth. The cow's sweet breath felt warm against his skin, and her eyelashes fluttered nervously. "Come, cow," he said, rubbing her shoulder. She took a step, and the holy man smiled at Mohan across her back. Mohan touched the cow's broad cheek to guide her toward the edge of the road.

Finally the cow shuffled out of their way. As Mohan settled back into his seat, Ba patted his knee and smiled. The driver picked up the handles again and it seemed only moments before they had reached the market. "Cloth and coriander spice," Mrs. Gandhi said, stepping out. "Help me remember, Mohan, potatoes and chickpeas and perhaps a new bangle bracelet, too."

He stared at stalls where they actually sold meat. Chickens clucked from small cages, dead ducks hung upside down, and the turbaned butcher hacked a bloody chunk off the skinned leg of a sheep. "Come, Mohan," Ba scolded. "That is not for us."

"Who can eat that?" Mohan asked, his stomach churning.

"Muslims. They do not believe in the holiness of every animal, as we do." She turned to a woman who had bought meat. "Good morning," Putlibai said to the Muslim woman. Mohan watched them chat together about the weather.

Mohan imagined the woman putting a piece

of animal in her mouth. She would chew it. Then she would swallow. He shuddered. "Mohan!" Putlibai's sharp voice broke through his thoughts. "Where are your manners?"

Mohan bowed and touched his head to the Muslim woman's feet. "I am honored to meet you," he said.

"And here is Mrs. Smythe," Putlibai said. Again, Mohan bowed his respect to an adult— but to an English woman whose feet were covered in shoes made from cow skin. He glanced at his mother to see if she knew about the leather shoes. She was smiling at him proudly. Mohan stood tall. He was proud that his mother had such varied and important friends.

"Will the rains be early again this year, do you think?" Putlibai was saying as the trio of women moved down the dusty street together. "I can't wait for monsoon season to arrive." They stopped by a vegetable-farmer's stall and began bargaining over the price of chickpeas and potatoes.

Finally, the bargaining seemed to be over.

"For the boy," the farmer said, wrapping a juicy slice of papaya in a banana leaf. He handed it to Mohandas. "Save it for your noon meal." Mohan's mouth watered at the thought of chewing the sweet, juicy fruit. His stomach grumbled. He wanted to hurry home where he could wash and say grace at the table and eat this treat.

The women weren't done talking, though. Now they were discussing where to find the finest cloth imported from England.

Mohan listened a few moments. Soon he began staring at a street sweeper. The old man dodged back and forth between carts and shoppers, his back bowed with age and the weight of stinking garbage in his pail. With his trowel, he scooped cow and donkey droppings off the dirt road, rotting scraps from the food stalls, and litter too slimy to identify. Mohan held his breath as the man neared him. The street sweeper set his bucket down and stopped a moment to stretch his back.

Mohan glanced at his mother. She was still

talking with a Muslim and an English woman. Ba wanted to be like her. "Good morning, sir." He stepped toward the street sweeper. "Do you think the rains will be early this year?"

The man stared for a moment, open-mouthed, then turned and scurried away. "Mohan!" Ba's furious voice cut through the noise of the crowd. "Get away from him!"

Suddenly Putlibai was dragging him back toward the rickshaw. "How could you do that?" she scolded. "He didn't touch you, did he?" Mohan watched his mother shudder with disgust. "That man is an Untouchable! Did his breath cross your skin? Did his shadow fall on you? Hurry, we'll get you home for a bath. How *could* you?"

As their driver began sprinting toward home, Mohan rubbed his arm where his mother's fingers had dug in. "Do you understand what happened?" Ba asked, her voice calmer. "You look so wise sometimes, I forget how young you are. You were born on October 2,

1869. . . . It is 1875, so you are only"—she paused—"a baby."

"Why is that man Untouchable?" Mohan asked, trying to sound old.

Beside him his mother shifted. "Untouchables are people who have the dirtiest jobs—jobs that have to be done—jobs no one else would want to do. They sweep streets, handle dead bodies, clean toilets, and worse. They live in filth and hunger."

"Are there Untouchable children?" Mohan asked.

"Of course," Ba said. "When a woman from the Untouchable caste has a child, it must do its god-given job too. We all must do our *dharma*, our duty." She looked at Mohan's face and smiled. "It isn't hopeless, little one. If an Untouchable lives a holy life and performs his duties carefully until he dies, his soul could return to live again in a higher caste."

Mohan thought for a few moments. "Does it work the other way? If I don't do what I am supposed to, could I come back as an Untouchable?"

"Yes," Ba said. "Or a cow, a snake, or even a dog. But that is why you *will* do your dharma, Mohan. You *will* follow the Hindu rules for living, get an education, have children, and support us when we get old. And that is why we teach you how to collect good *karma*. You gather karma from what you do. Just this morning, you gathered good karma by obeying me, by helping a cow sacred to Vishnu, and by being polite to your elders. That goodness will come back to you sometime in this life, or in your next one."

"What happened when I spoke to an Untouchable?"

Putibai's mouth tightened. "Bad karma," she said, her voice dark.

Mohan remembered the smell of the street sweeper's bucket. "How can I get rid of it?"

"You must balance it by doing great good," Ba said. "Stop!" she called to the driver.

"Mohan, quick. There is a holy man." Mohan followed her glance to a naked man padding down the street. His body was smeared with mud, and mud caked his straggly hair.

Mohan stared. He had been told that these wanderers had given up their homes and families as well as their clothes. They walked from shrine to shrine throughout India, praying night and day. They ate only what was given to them. Mohan looked down at the banana leaf package in his hands and glanced at Ba. Then he jumped out of the rickshaw and handed the holy man his treat.

Mohan darted back to the rickshaw. "He didn't give me a blessing," he told his mother. "He didn't even say thank you."

"Perhaps he gave up speech, too. That way his mind can concentrate on prayer," Ba said as the rickshaw rolled on toward home. "He must be very holy."

At home, Ba urged Mohan to hurry inside and take his clothes off. "You will wash," she said, "vigorously. Then stop at our shrine to light a candle to Vishnu before you come to the table."

Mohan scurried over to the men's side of the great Gandhi house. His five uncles and boy cousins, his brothers, and the families' male servants lived there. Mohan didn't stop to talk with anyone. He washed and dressed again in a loose cotton shirt and trousers. Then Mohandas chose a scented twig to scrub his teeth and gums, and rinsed his mouth the number of times required by Hindu practice. Sometimes this ceremony seemed to take forever, but now it made his mouth—and his head—feel right again.

He crossed into the common side of the house, used by men and women, and stepped into the household shrine. Ba was there, her head bowed. Incense filled the air. The statue of Vishnu sat on its shelf, as alive and powerful-looking as the god himself. Pictures of Vishnu in his other forms circled the altar: as a baby, as a lover, as a warrior—all beautiful, all holy. The other gods and goddesses—the sword-carrying Kali, jolly Ganesha, playful Krishna, dancing Shiva—they too, had their place. Mohan stepped forward to light a candle and wave it before the display. Its flame made the gilded pictures sparkle with power.

When Mohan closed his eyes and bowed before the altar, he could still see the sparkles before his eyes.

Railit, Mohandas's ten-year-old sister, stepped quietly behind them. "We can eat," she said. In the front hall, Mohan's father was just saying good-bye to his clients. *"Namaste,"* he repeated, bowing his head over folded hands as each left. *"Namaste.* From the God within me to the God within you."

The guests bowed low. "Namaste, Bapu," Mohan said carefully. Sometimes his father was kindly, sometimes impatient. Mohan grinned as Kaba Gandhi laughed with joy.

"My boy!" he said. "The flower of my old age."

Mohan looked at his father quickly. Yes, Kaba Gandhi's hair was gray at the temples, and his great bristly mustache had gray hairs. His face was far more wrinkled than Ba's too. "Are you old, Bapu?"

Kaba laughed again as they walked into the dining room. "Not with you to keep things lively here," he said, and patted Mohan's head. "And with a beautiful, saintly wife like Putlibai—my fourth—I might just live forever."

Ba motioned for everyone to sit on the floor around bowls fragrant with curry and heaped with rice. The Gandhi brothers, eight-year-old Karsandas and twelve-year-old Lakshmidas folded easily into their places. For the first time Mohan noticed that Kaba sighed as he settled to the floor.

After Kaba said a thank-you to Mother Earth for sharing her bounty with them, one of the servants put food on the banana leaf in front of each family member. Mohan leaned on his left hand—the one saved for dirty uses—and scooped up food with his right hand.

"Bapu," he said between bites, "I like it that you and Ba are friendly with everyone. Except," he corrected himself quickly, "Untouchables."

"I need to do business with all kinds," Bapu said. "And they all are friendly with me."

"Everyone respects your father," Putlibai said, staring proudly at her husband. "He is known everywhere for being honest and fair."

"Oh, Ba," Railit said, touching her mother's hand. "I only hope to be as good a wife to my husband as you are to Bapu."

"You as a *wife*?" Karsandas choked on his food, and Lakshmidas pounded him on his back. "*You?*"

"Silence!" Kaba roared. The boys looked everywhere but at their sister, who blushed pink. Mohan shifted closer to his mother. "All four of you will marry the people we have chosen. We will pick your wedding days. You all will be good to your mates for life."

*My wife is already chosen?* Mohan thought. He looked at his siblings. They all seemed to be thinking too—about wives and weddings and plans already settled. Mohan hoped his future wife was someone like Ba. He stuffed another mound of curry into his mouth. He did not dare ask about his chosen mate now that Bapu's mood had turned sour.

Dinner passed in silence. Ba prayed a final "thank-you" for the food, then everyone scuttled away. Mohan headed toward the kitchen, then out the back doorway. Father Sun's heat gnawed at Mohan through the thin cotton shirt. Its glare blinded his eyes. Like Ba, Mohan wished for the rainy season to start and cool Mother Earth.

"Watch your step!" a breathless voice said behind him. Mohan froze, waiting until his eyes cleared. A cobra lay sunning itself on the path. "Don't hurt him!" the kitchen maid said.

*"Ahisma,"* Mohandas breathed, stepping back carefully.

"Right." The maid said, "We welcome him with saucers of milk. He does his duty, eating the rats and mice that dare to come near our kitchen. We do not hurt him. He does not bite us."

"Ahisma," Mohan said, thinking aloud. "This snake is as sacred as the old cow. As me." Suddenly he wondered what the snake had done in his past life to deserve being a cobra this time.

Mohandas closed his sun-stung eyes. In prayer, he promised Vishnu he would always do his dharma. And he would collect every bit of good karma he could in this lifetime.

CHAPTER 2
# POWER

"England is the most powerful country in the world," the teacher announced. "King Edward is the most powerful ruler." Mohan squirmed uncomfortably in the hot classroom. His father was a ruler too. *Thwack!* The teacher smacked the stick against a map hanging against a wall. All the boys jumped.

"Here you are in India. India is ruled by England." Mr. Tuttle-Swain hit the map again. *Thwack. Thwack!* "Scotland and Ireland are also under British rule." Again the pointer moved. *Thwack!* "Canada. Part of the British Empire." The pointer moved on. "Thwack. South Africa." Pause. *Thwack. Thwack.* "Australia. New Zealand." The list went on and on. With each slap of the pointer, Mohan felt smaller.

"England's navy rules the seas. Our laws and courts govern hundreds and millions of people." Mohan thought quickly. Porbandar had only five thousand people. Perhaps Bapu wasn't powerful after all? *No.* He clenched his fists. Some king in a country far, far away had power over all these countries? Over Bapu? He glared at the map and felt his fists clench. *Ahisma,* he reminded himself, and felt his temper cool.

He was seven now. He should have better control.

Mr. Tuttle-Swain fanned himself and looked over the class. "Does everyone understand what I've been saying?" he asked. "Mohandas Gandhi, are you having a problem?"

Mohan stood up to answer. "No sir," he said. "I understand English very well now."

"You are quite a student," the teacher said. He looked at the others. "You should all model yourselves after young Gandhi, here." Mohan shrank back to his seat. Now all his classmates would hate him.

Thunder rolled in the distance. "Chatmuras!" one student said. "The rains are coming!" "At last!" "The monsoon!" Everyone stirred restlessly.

"Attention, students!" Mr. Tuttle-Swain called out. "We will now turn to writing and spelling." He looked around, and Mohan tried to be invisible. "Mohandas Gandhi, will you pass out the slates?"

Mohan slunk to the back of the room and picked up a pile of slates and pieces of chalk. Almost every student rolled his eyes or hissed as he handed them their supplies.

"Eyes here," the teacher called. He wrote a list of English words on the board and said them distinctly. "Great Britain. Empire," he said. "Britannia. Subjects. That is, not like the subjects we study here at school," Mr. Tuttle-Swain explained. "A subject is a person under the power of another ruler. We all are subjects of the queen. And India is a subject nation." He stepped back and looked at the list. "The British government here is called the Raj." He wrote this on the board too.

Inside the classroom the sound of chalk scraping on slates hissed like rain all around Mohan. Outside, thunder rolled again, louder. The sky darkened. *Chatmuras,* Mohan thought. Rainy season. He couldn't wait!

"That's only five words." The teacher wiped his sweaty forehead with a handkerchief. He smoothed his mustache. "You should have ten spelling words. Church of England," he wrote. "Christian." Mohan fought against his temper again.

His father would allow Muslims and other Hindus into his home office, but not Christians. "Christians always try to make you change to their religion," Kaba would say. "Their religion is fine—for them. They should keep it." Mohan listened to see what the teacher would say next.

A sudden crack of thunder made everyone jump. Then rain slammed against the windows. It roared on the tin roof. Outside, all the sunbaked buildings steamed. Mr. Tuttle-Swain looked at his class full of boys lined up by the windows. "Go home," he said quietly. "School is out—but just for today."

The room was empty before he could say more. Children from all the other classes were racing out too. Rain—cool, sweet rain—poured over everyone. Thunder rumbled and lightning snapped in the air but no one took cover. Instead, they stood with arms outstretched, letting the monsoon rains rinse the sticky sweat out of their hair and clothes.

The dusty schoolyard flooded. A hundred bare feet squished dust and water into pale, sticky mud. The cool goo was inches deep and perfect for kicking onto classmates.

Mohan eased his way past the worst of the riotous crowd. No one thought to call him "teacher's favorite." They were all too busy celebrating. None of the bullies were interested in him today either. Mohan snuck through back streets where water ran like brown rivers.

He hurried home. Ba had told the children she would have an announcement when

Chatmuras began. And Mohandas wanted to talk with his father about the British Raj.

A servant handed him a towel as he entered his house. Mohan wiped his head, then his feet. He glanced at the mat where visitors were supposed to leave their shoes. It was empty. Perhaps Bapu was alone? Mohan knocked at the door of his father's study and pushed it open. Kaba Gandhi was standing at the window, staring out at the rain. He looked just like a schoolboy, Mohan thought, but only for a moment.

"Bapu! I have something to ask." Mohan caught his breath. "Um, Namaste, Bapu," he said. He walked closer and bowed to touch his head to his father's feet.

"Namaste," his father answered with a smile. "Why such a hurry?"

"The teacher today. He talked about the British Empire and the Raj here in India. Is it true? But *you* are in charge of Porbandar, aren't you?" Mohandas stopped. "Not some faraway king."

"What gets into you, little one? Questions—always questions!" He ruffled Mohan's hair. "I've never known a child like you." Bapu turned and looked out at the rain again.

"This is important," Mohan said.

"Indeed, it is," his father answered. "Perhaps we can sit down together with some tea and talk." Kaba pointed at a mat beside a low platform covered with papers. This was where Bapu did official dewan business! Mohan sat down cross-legged and tried to remember if he had ever talked with his father alone. The house was always full of family, friends and guests, brothers, cousins, and businessmen. Mohan could barely breathe as his father ordered the servant to bring tea and sweets for two. Bapu slowly eased himself to the mat on the other side of the desk.

"The English, you ask," he began. "The English. They first came here as traders about two hundred and fifty years ago." He took a deep breath. "They are clever, these English. They worked their way into our society. We

Indians have an ancient culture, but we did not see what the newcomers were doing. They gained political power. They brought in soldiers to control us. Approximately one hundred years ago, they took over all two million square miles of India. They formed a government, the Raj, to rule India."

Lakshmidas stormed into the room. "There you are, Mohan!" he said, then stopped. "Bapu, excuse me. Namaste. But we have been so worried! Little brother, why aren't you out playing with us in the rain?"

The servant entered with a tray of teacups and honey-soaked candies. "What is happening here?" Lakshmidas demanded. "I am the one who is about to have the ceremony for my first shaving. Yet you choose to sit with the baby of the family?"

"Sit down, Lakshmidas," Bapu said calmly. He took a sip of tea. "Mohan doesn't understand about the Raj." He motioned the servant to bring more tea. "Can you explain it?"

"England rules 'British India,'" Lakshmidas

said. "They make all the laws there. British governors enforce them in British courts. The British viceroy is their ruler. He takes orders only from the English king."

"But that isn't true here, Bapu, is it?" Mohan struggled to swallow a candy before he went on. "We have a prince. I've seen him and he is Indian."

"Porbandar is a 'native state,'" Bapu explained. "There are dozens of native states, each ruled by a prince. Each one has a dewan like me to keep things running smoothly. But the princes—and the dewans—have to please the local British officials—the Raj."

The tea in Mohan's mouth suddenly tasted sour. "That means . . ."

"Mohandas!" They all turned toward Mrs. Gandhi's voice at the doorway. Ba could not enter the men's rooms, but her anger could. "Mohan, where have you been? And Lakshmidas, you had to know your younger brother would be frantic when both of you went missing."

Lakshmidas jumped to his feet. "Forgive me, Ba. I will come to him now."

"I too will come," Mohan said. He needed to think about what he had heard.

"Why don't we all have tea and sweets on the porch?" Mr. Gandhi suggested. "The air will be cool there now." He gestured to the servant. "We can all celebrate the coming of Chatmuras together."

"But—" Ba began to protest. Bapu cut her off.

"Wife," he said flatly, "we will meet on the porch." Mohan watched his mother bow her head and leave the room. Indian men had power over their wives, he knew. But he did not often see his father use it. For a moment, he felt bad for his mother. Then he hurried out to the porch.

"There, isn't this grand?" Mr. Gandhi said as his family sat on the mats around a dinner. Beyond the eaves, the rain still poured. The air was mild and soft and clean-smelling. "What a relief from the heat!"

The boys all agreed. Railit said, "I lost a shoe in the mud." When Lakshmidas laughed, she shot back, "The shoe matched my favorite sari, the pale green one."

Mohan pictured his sister wrapped in yards of the green silk, looking graceful and grown up. "I'll look for it with you," he offered.

"Be careful you don't lose Mohandas in the mud too," Karsandas said. "I did." He made a sad face at his brother.

Lakshmidas laughed. "I know how to find Mohandas. Just look for a tray of sweets!"

While Mohan tried to protest that he wasn't greedy, Bapu raised his hand. Immediately all were silent.

"Why have you eaten nothing?" Kaba asked his wife. "This is a celebration."

"I am celebrating Chatmuras in my own way. I made a promise to Vishnu. For him, I will eat only every other day while the rains fall."

"You will eat one day and fast the next?" Karsandas asked.

"Won't you be hungry?" Mohan said. He thought a moment. "How is that a gift to a God?"

"It is a sacrifice. It will prove I love Him more than my own comfort."

"Won't you be hungry?" Lakshmidas asked.

"I have power over my urges," Ba said. "We all do."

"It is tiresome to be married to a saint," Bapu said. His words sounded impatient, but his eyes were full of love for his wife.

"Children!" Mr. Gandhi stood at the edge of the beach. It was the dry season again. Eight-year-old Mohandas was flying a kite he had made. Lakshmidas and Karsandas were wrestling in the sand. Railit was bathing in the waves with her friends. Their saris spread in the water like lilies on a pond. Bapu had to call many times before all of his children gathered.

"What is it, Bapu?" Mohan asked.

"I have been told to move," Mr. Gandhi said. "We are going inland to Rajkot."

"We can't leave the old house!" Lakshmidas said. "Gandhis have lived in it for generations."

"But my friends!" Railit's eyes filled with tears.

Mohan watched a ship sailing free on the ocean. Its sails were blindingly white in the tropical sun. Its topmast flew the British flag. "Rajkot is a hundred miles from the beach!" Lakshmidas whined.

"A hundred and twenty," Bapu corrected.

As they walked home, the children kept complaining: "We have a school here." "Ba knows the merchants at the marketplace here." "I'll lose my place on the cricket team." "Can we bring all my saris along?" Only Mohan was silent.

When the others had gone into the house to get hugs from Ba, Mohan hung back. "What happened?" he asked his father. "Why Rajkot? It is a far smaller state than Porbandar. Will you still be dewan?"

Bapu rested his hand on Mohan's head. "You always see right to the heart of things, don't you?" He sighed. "That can't be easy for one so young." He sighed again. "We go to Rajkot because the British say so. The prince in Rajkot needs a dewan like me to help straighten things out there." He brushed a sandal in the dusty courtyard. "'This is an honor,' they said." He paused. "'You are fair. You are honest. You are the best dewan in all the native states.' That is what they said."

"You do not take this as an honor," Mohandas said. That was clear from his father's voice.

"I must leave everything I have built here," Bapu said slowly. "And I am too old to start again."

*My father is powerless!* Mohan thought. *And the British have too much power.*

Mohandas had his eighth birthday party in Rajkot. The house was smaller. There was no sea-smell on the breeze. But there were saris and cricket teams there, new friends and a school. The prince there needed Bapu—and Bapu did his dharma. The dry season was just as hot as at home. Soon everyone was looking forward to Chatmuras again.

"This year," Bapu announced, "in Vishnu's honor, I will eat only when the sun shines." Her children were silent. This was serious. Monsoon season meant endless gray skies and day after day of rain. When would they see the sun? Would Ba starve herself to death?

When there had been a break in the weather, they ran home from school. "Did she eat? Did Ba eat?" they asked the servants. When they saw a glimpse of sun while playing, they ran indoors. "Ba, you can eat now!"

"I must see this sun for myself," Mrs. Gandhi would answer. She followed them to the yard. If the sun was still shining, she broke her fast with a meal. If clouds had swept back over the sky, she said, "That does not matter. God did not want me to eat today."

Mohandas could see the fight in her eyes. Ba was hungry. She was losing weight. Her elbows and cheekbones seemed to get sharp. Her temper clearly did. Then she began to lose the energy to shop all day or bustle around the new house. But Ba did not give in. Mohan admired her strength. She was only a woman, but she was so powerful!

# CHAPTER 3
# THE SURPRISE

"I am troubled about school today," Mohan confessed to his mother.

"Trouble? You? You are thirteen now. You are old enough to know better," Ba scolded as she folded laundry. Then she looked at her son's face. "Mohan, tell me about it."

"I did not get *in* trouble, Ba. Well, I guess I did—but that is not what troubles me." Mohan stumbled for the right words. Mrs. Gandhi kept doing her chores, waiting silently. "The teacher scolded me because I missed the word 'kettle' on our spelling test. He said I pulled down the whole class average. And he said it in front of the others."

"This does not sound like your teacher." Mrs. Gandhi folded a pale blue sari. "Why did it matter so to him?" Mohandas shook his head. "Think, Mohan," Ba insisted. "What could have made one missed spelling word so important?" She reached for another sari.

"The school overseer—the English one—was visiting Alfred Boys High School last week." Mohan folded a towel to help his mother. "I knew that. A less-than-perfect average made him look bad to his boss."

"Then this is not your problem, son."

"But it is, Ba. During the test the teacher kept pointing to my desk mate's paper. He wanted me to copy the correct spelling. But I refused. I disobeyed. It isn't honest to cheat, is it, Ba? Even if a teacher suggests it?"

Putlibai Gandhi put down her laundry. "Mohandas, I am proud of you. Just because someone is in charge doesn't mean he is always right. You were wise, and brave too, to do the right thing instead of obeying."

Mohan folded a towel angrily. He did not look at his mother when he said, "Everyone in class is mad at me."

"This is like karma, Mohan. You don't always get rewarded for doing good right away. Sometimes it takes years. Sometimes your reward comes in the next life. But it *does* come."

They worked silently together for a few moments. Then Mohan laughed. "You mean God won't throw me a party every time I do something right?"

Ba laughed too. Then she straightened up. "That reminds me. Mohan, your father and I *will* be throwing a party for you soon. A big one. We hadn't meant to tell you for a few weeks. . . ." Mrs. Gandhi motioned to a servant to carry the pile of folded laundry away. "When he is ready, your father will tell you and Karsandas," she said. No matter how much Mohan begged, his mother refused to say more.

His brothers were no help. "I don't know what she is talking about," Karsandas swore. Lakshmidas, now married and working as a lawyer's assistant, wouldn't tell. Mohan could not ask his sister, Raliat, what was going on. She had married too, and had gone to live with her new husband's family back in Porbandar. The servants giggled and covered their mouths when he asked what was going on.

Something big was happening. The answer seemed to come quickly. Both Mohan and Karsandas, and even their cousin, were initiated.

"We are of the Vaishyas," Bapu said. "Our caste produces tradespeople, artisans, farmers, and businesspeople like us. Ours is a caste of high honor."

Mohan knew that rulers and the soldiers protecting them came from the top caste, the Kshatriya. Scholars and priests came mostly from the next caste, the Brahmins. His people, the Vaishyas, were next. Until now, he had not thought of them as so honorable.

Of course they were far, far above the Shudra caste of Untouchables. Mohan shuddered at the thought.

Bapu, as head of the household, sat in a circle with the boys and instructed them in the traditions of the Vaishyas. Other days, a friend of the family who was a Brahmin priest joined them on the floor. He told them of their vows and special prayers as adult Hindu men. They must, he said, observe the religious laws, marry, raise children to be good Hindus, and care for their parents. Or they could choose to give up this path and live their lives as wandering holy men.

"I do not choose that life," Mohan said. His brother and cousin agreed.

Karsandas turned to Mohan and whispered, "We will soon be real *men*, little brother!"

Mohan looked at Karsandas's smooth cheeks. "You have not had the ceremony of first shaving yet," he said. Karsandas stared at him in disgust. Mohan sat taller. "We will be men," he agreed.

"Hush!" the priest said. Bapu looked at them crossly. From that moment on, Mohan listened silently. This was serious. At the initiation ceremony, he took off his shirt. A string was draped across his left shoulder and tied on his right side. Prayers and blessings were made over him. When he put his shirt back on, the string was still there to remind him that he was a man, a man of the Vaishya. "You can never take off that string, just like you can never leave our caste," Bapu reminded him.

Mohan knew now that Bapu wore a string. All the grown men of the top three castes wore this reminder beneath their clothing. Karsandas showed off his string to anyone who would look. Mohan kept his hidden at the great feast that was held in their honor. "I am glad to know the surprise that Ba and Bapu were planning for us," Karsandas said.

But the gardeners kept planting even more flowers in the courtyards. Servants hung every rug outside one day and beat the dust out of them. Painters repainted the walls inside the house. Roofers replaced the missing tiles. Ba chose four new saris at the market. A tailor measured Mohan and Karsandas and a cousin too, and then left.

Everything was getting ready—but if not to

celebrate the boys becoming men, for what?

One day, Mr. Gandhi called the boys into his office together; his sons plus their fourteen-year-old cousin and his father. The boys sat fidgeting on a mat. Lakshmidas stood winking and smirking at them. Finally, Mr. Gandhi cleared his throat. "We have decided," he said, "that the three of you will be married next month."

Mohan froze. His father went on, talking about how it would be cheaper to throw the ceremonies for three and how everything was almost ready.

"Bapu," Mohan interrupted. "I am getting *married*?"

Lakshmidas burst out laughing. "Weren't you listening, little one? Soon you will be a husband!"

"I will have a wife?" Mohan sputtered. "Now?"

Lakshmidas roared with laughter. Even Bapu and his brother were laughing. Karsandas and his cousin started making fun of

Mohandas. "Who, me?" Karsandas said. The cousin dove at him and they began wrestling. The room was full of excitement, but Mohan still struggled to understand.

"Who will I marry?" he demanded. "What do I do as a married man? Do I still go to school?"

As the others struggled to get themselves back under control, Mohan got his answers. "Your wife was chosen back when you were both seven, back in Porbandar," Bapu said. "We'll try and make sure you get to meet her before the ceremony."

Lakshmidas told him to buy a pamphlet at the market on how to treat a wife. The men looked at one another and began chuckling. His uncle said, "Mohan, you were married in your past lives. Trust me. Your body will remember what to do with a wife."

"I want to do this right," Mohan said. He looked around the room for help. Lakshmidas met his eyes. "My wife would be happy to explain things to you from the woman's point of view," he offered. Mohan smiled his thanks.

"And of course you'll go to school," Bapu said. "I expect your grades to rise since you'll be studying more at night." Again, the men's laughter rose.

"Our brides are in Porbandar?" Karsandas said. "That means our wedding procession will go for a hundred miles!" He leaned over and dangled his arm in front of his face. "I get to ride the elephant!" he claimed.

"No, I ride!" his cousin argued, and jumped onto his back.

"One elephant?" Mohan asked. "No! Three elephants for three bridegrooms!" He waved a fake trunk in front of his own nose and charged into the other boys. They all fell to the floor together, giggling.

Mohan thought what Lakshmidas's wife told him sounded like another game, though a strange one. He liked what he read much better. The pamphlets he bought described how a proper husband was the ruler of his wife.

Mohan knew what it felt like to have bullies pushing him around. It would be nice to be making the rules for someone else for a change.

His mother even told him his new wife's name. "Her name is Kasturbai, Mohan. Kasturbai Makanji," Ba said. "You will learn that name well, for you will be married to her for the rest of your life. She must be faithful to you and you to her."

"Kasturbai?" Mohan tried the feel of her name in his mouth. "Kasturbai Gandhi."

"Your love will grow as the two of you do." Ba smiled to herself. "You will bring me many grandchildren and after I am gone, you will grow old together."

After that, Mohan wanted to go and play with the boys outdoors.

The month sped by. At last it was time for the boys to travel to Porbandar. There were no elephants. Camels and carriages decorated with live flowers, and wagons filled with gifts for the bride's families, stretched in a long line down the road. "Go without me," said Bapu, who had to stay at the last minute. "The prince has just given me extra paperwork to do. He will give me a fast carriage when I am done. I should be just a day behind you."

Bapu had not arrived yet when Mohan met Kasturbai's father. His new father-in-law recited prayers and washed the dirt of the journey from Mohan's feet. Mohan fought to not giggle as the man's fingers tickled his toes. Then his father-in-law fed him a special sweet paste of honey and yogurt and oil to welcome him.

Next, Mohan got dressed in one of his new outfits to see his bride. Kasturbai sat in a chair facing him, her body swathed in silk and shiny new jewelry. Mohan stared at her dark brown eyes and tried to tell what kind of a person she was. She was not ugly, and her skin looked healthy and clear. She didn't seem shy, and she might even have smiled as her father cleared his throat. Mohan jumped, realizing it was time for him to recite a prayer. He asked the gods to remove any faults in his wife-to-be. He begged them to make her loyal and long-lived and give them lots of children. Though his mouth spoke to the gods, his eyes were fixed on Kasturbai. He couldn't remember ever having seen her back when he'd lived in Porbandar. He tried to imagine her carrying a baby, or old.

A long blade of grass was pressed into his hand, and Mohan rose thankfully. There was more for him to do in this ceremony—much more. He gently wiped Kasturbai's eyebrows with the grass, as if he were chasing away all flaws. She seemed to be trying not to giggle, and her eyes crinkled in a real smile. *She is ticklish*, he thought. This was going to be fun! Once he had wiped her faults away, he threw the grass behind his bride.

"Where *is* Bapu?" Mohan asked his relatives as he was led into a changing room. "I should not do this without his blessing." Too many things—important things—seemed to be happening in a blur.

"Your father has arrived," an uncle said.

"But you must not be surprised when you see him." Mohan stared at his uncle. "Your father rushed too fast to get here in time. His carriage flipped over," the uncle explained. Then he added quickly, "Bapu is fine. But you must change now. Kasturbai is waiting to make her vows with you."

There was no time to see his father. Mohan had to change clothes again. Part of him wanted to argue, "But I want to see Bapu!" Another part tried to remember all the lines he had to repeat in the ceremony. He had practiced them at home until they were perfect. Now his mind was confused and his fingers fumbled with his clothing.

"It is time for you to tie your bride," his older brother prompted. Mohan hurried into the front room. His eyes searched for Bapu. There he was. Mohan had to stare. Bapu seemed to have bandages everywhere! He nodded at Mohan and pointed across the room.

Kasturbai was waiting there with her family. Mohan tried to focus on her and not worry about his father. He smiled at Kasturbai as he tied the rope around her waist. She did not meet his eyes. Mohan led her toward a fire lit on a burner in the center of the room. They sat together on a fresh grass mat. Mohan glanced at his father, and then recited three ancient prayers to give Kasturbai strength, beauty, and youth.

Now she looked right at him. Mohan's breath stopped. This was real. This girl was marrying him forever. Who *was* she?

They recited more prayers. Then it was time for Kasturbai to enter the Gandhi household. Ba had made sure the family's grindstone was packed along with the bride gifts. It sat next to the sacred fire. Mohan led Kasturbai to it, and she stepped three times on its rough surface pledging herself to the service of the Gandhis. She, too, knew her lines. Mohan was glad.

Then it was time to walk around the fire together. Seven times they circled the flame. There were seven promises and seven prayers to go with the movements. Mohan began the first circle, his right hand wrapped around Kasturbai's. Everyone around them was so serious, he felt a giggle rising in his throat. Then in his belly. He had to swallow hard to keep the laughter inside. Didn't anyone see how silly this was? His eyes met his mother's. She was crying! Mohan's giggles died.

Ba had walked these same steps with Bapu. Every married couple had. *I have walked these same steps in other lives,* Mohan thought. The ancient vows came to his lips easily now. They were sweet and they were forever. He had said them before in other lives. He would say them again in other lives to come. Mohan felt dizzy.

Kasturbai's hand squeezed his. Suddenly he was back in the room, marrying *this* girl for *this* lifetime. He smiled at her in thanks. Now, over the incense, he could smell the delicious feast to come. He felt the heat of the flames. And the sense of the words he was saying came back to him.

There were more prayers. Melted butter

was poured on the sacred fire as an offering. Rice was burned too. Finally Mohan untied the rope binding him to Kasturbai. He knew that the ties between them now were far stronger than rope. The room burst into noise as everyone offered their blessings. Kasturbai's mother hugged her. Ba rose and limped a few steps, but Mohan pushed through the crowd to greet her. Ba congratulated him as if he were a man. Mohan took a deep breath. It was over.

His stomach growled and Mohan looked toward the feast room. All of his favorite treats were there. He could eat as much as he liked today—and he would get to eat first. That was how it had worked at his brother's wedding the day before. "Did you forget something?" someone said as he hurried toward the food.

Mohan looked up in surprise. "Your wife," the stranger said, and laughter broke out all around them. Mohan looked around the room quickly. "She's over there," the man said kindly, giving him a gentle shove in the right direction. The man, Mohan realized, had to be one of Kasturbai's relatives. *My* relative now, Mohan corrected himself. He would have to learn all their names and who they all were. Mohan felt worn out by all the emotions of the day—until he saw Kasturbai's smiling face.

"Shall we eat?" she said when he reached her side. Mohan grinned in response, and she followed him to the feast.

That night, Mohan and Kasturbai, their stomachs bulging with sweets, were left alone together. They talked for hours, getting to know each other. They cuddled together. *Forever.* The word kept ringing in Mohan's ears. Kasturbai was his, day and night, forever. Finally, exhausted, they slept.

The next day, Karsandas had his wedding. The following day, it was their cousin's turn. At last, they packed everything up—including the three new wives—and headed home. Flowers pelted them as they left. Crowds applauded the newlyweds in villages all the way to Rajkot. The servants greeted them with flowers and cheers, too. Those servants had been busy.

Mohan led his wife to his bedroom and stopped. Everything was gone. "Your things are in the married couple's part of the house, now," a servant told him. He led the bride and groom to a new room. The sleeping mat was wider. There was more space all about and a window, too. Chests stood ready for clothing—far more clothing than Mohan had. Filmy curtains billowed in the breeze.

Mohan remembered the rules he had read for being a proper husband. He straightened up. "You will sleep on the side with no window," he said firmly. Kasturbai nodded. "You will rub my feet before we go to bed," he said. Kasturbai nodded again. Mohan grinned to himself. Being a husband was going to be fun. "Kasturbai—" he began again, but she interrupted.

"If you do not mind," she said, "I should go to the women's side of the house. I must wash the dirt of the road from my body. Then I should prepare dinner with the women." She looked at him out of the corner of her eye. "I know how you like to eat."

Mohan felt cheated. "Very well," he said. "Go. But do not interrupt me like that again." He watched her swish out of the door. Her body was so graceful in her sari, he thought. When his eyes fell on a pile of books, he sighed. There was homework to do, lots of it. He had missed days of school while he was away getting married. Mohan picked up a mathematics book and sat cross-legged on the floor to get back to work.

# CHAPTER 4
# PLAYING HUSBAND

Every day when Mohan got home from school, he called for Kasturbai. Wherever she was in the woman's side of the house, she would come running. Mohan loved that. She listened to whatever had happened in his day. Sometimes they went outside to fly kites. Other times they walked along the street while Mohan talked. He stood tall beside her. Under his shirt he wore the string of a man. Kasturbai wore the red dot of a married woman on her forehead for all to see.

"Shall we read together this afternoon?" Mohan said one day. "I am falling behind in my homework."

Kasturbai turned her face away.

"Don't be like that," Mohan scolded. "My problem is partly your fault, anyway. You want me to spend every afternoon with you, and the nights . . ." He let the word trail off and watched Kasturbai's face blush. "I awaken tired in the morning because of you. I am too tired after dinner to do my homework then. When am I supposed to get it done?"

"We do not have to spend every afternoon together," Kasturbai said softly. "I could do my part to help the women cook."

"You will read with me," Mohan said firmly. "We can sit together on the porch while I get caught up on my assignments."

"No," Kasturbai said.

"You are my wife!" he said sharply. "You cannot deny me!" Mohan had been practicing those words. They came from the book on how to be a husband. He watched to see how they would work.

Kasturbai looked furious for a moment. Then she nodded her head. "I will sit on the porch with you," she said. Moments later they met on the second-floor porch. They sat side by side on cushions on the floor.

Mohan began reading. He looked from his reading book to Kasturbai's. She was busy sewing a tear in a pair of his trousers.

Mohan felt his face flush. Why would she not obey him? "I told you to read with me, Kasturbai. You cannot deny me," Mohan said threateningly.

Kasturbai put the needle down. "I can't read with you, husband, because I can't read."

One look at her face told Mohan she was telling the truth. "Did you not go to school?"

Kasturbai shook her head. "A girl has no need of schooling."

"But you *must* read," Mohan said. "I will teach you how." For weeks he tried to show Kasturbai how to read. She said she was trying. She stared at the letters he showed her. She repeated their names aloud. But when Mohan asked her to read the alphabet back to him, Kasturbai only looked confused. Mohan said rude and cruel things to her, but it didn't seem to help. She could not seem to remember the alphabet no matter how many times he repeated it to her.

Mohan got even further behind in his homework. He could not get his wife to do this simple thing for him. They argued and Mohan got so angry, he sometimes refused to speak to her for days. Finally he gave up. "Perhaps you will learn in the summer when I have more time to teach you," he said.

"Perhaps," she answered. It did not sound like she meant it at all. "May I go and work with the women now?"

"Yes," Mohan growled, and went back to his overdue homework. His teachers would not take the excuse of a disobedient wife. Other students seemed to look down on him—for letting his grades slip, for being tired and cranky, and even for being married so young.

"Childhood marriages should be outlawed," Sheik Mehtab announced one day as the school boys lined up to enter the building. Sheik was one of the most popular boys at the high school. He was older than Mohan and in class with Karsandas. Sheik was tall and athletic. He was handsome and got good grades. Mohan would admire him—if he wasn't a Muslim.

"Let it go, Mohan. That is just how Muslims feel," Bapu told him that night at dinner. He scooped a big helping of spicy potatoes and cauliflower from a dish and passed it to his wife. "They make up a quarter of our country. Muslims and Hindus all get along together, though they have very different feelings about many things."

"They eat meat," Kasturbai said, and shuddered visibly.

"They do not read our holy books," Mohan said.

"Have you forgotten, son?" Ba challenged. "In our temple, the priest reads from the Muslim's holy Koran as well as from our ancient holy books of the Hindus. There is wisdom in both religions."

Mohan was embarrassed. As a boy he had gone to temple several times a week with his mother. He could quote from the Koran as easily as he could from the ancient Veda and the *Bhagavad Gita*. He had never read either scripture, but he had heard them since before he could remember. "Sorry, Ba," he said quietly.

Bapu cleared his throat. "Kasturbai's parents have written to me. They would like their daughter back for a few months."

"No," Mohan said. He stared at his wife. "She can't leave me."

"It will be only until the next rainy season," Ba said gently. She looked at Mohan's face. "Most young brides split their time between homes and husband. We agreed to this."

"*I* didn't agree," Mohan said.

"Your parents and hers feel you could use some time apart," Ba said. Her voice was gentle, but Mohan felt he had been scolded again. And they were taking his wife away! He looked to Kasturbai for help, but she was smiling as she never did anymore. She *wanted* to go home! Mohan blinked back sudden tears.

★　★　★　★

When the carriage brought Kasturbai back months later, she looked older. Mohan had practiced a speech to welcome her home and remind her that she was his wife. Instead, he stood, open-mouthed. He had not remembered how pretty she was, or how graceful.

His arms reached out to her, but then he let them drop. How could he touch this lovely young woman? Kasturbai did not seem to know what to say either.

"Get her bags!" Ba scolded a servant. "Mohan, where are your manners? Help her down from the carriage. You are her husband! Take care of her." Mohan saw a flash of impatience cross Kasturbai's face. Then his wife stepped out of the carriage without help.

"It is good to see you, my husband," she said. "I have missed you."

"I have missed you, too." Mohan heard the words tumble out of his mouth. "I'm caught up in my classes now. At the end of the last school year I even won a prize. This year the teachers think I am smart." He took a breath and began babbling again. "I cleaned up our room and lit incense in there for you. You can have the window side of the bed now. I can't wait to . . ." he stopped himself before he could say "cuddle with you." Instead, he finished the sentence with ". . . fly kites with you."

"I have much to tell you, too," Kasturbai said with a smile. "Shall we go in now?" Ba laughed as Mohan grabbed Kasturbai's arm and led her into the Gandhi house. He left for school that day, full of joy and excitement.

The joy didn't last long. By afternoon, Kasturbai seemed to look at him as if he were a little boy now instead of as her husband. That wasn't fair. They were both fourteen. And he wasn't a little boy. He wore the string to prove it.

He heard that Kasturbai had spent hours praying with Ba in the household shrine that day. Now they seemed more like girlfriends than in-laws. The Gandhi family laughed at dinner when Kasturbai repeated servant talk she had overheard. She bubbled over with funny stories of life at her old house too.

"You are a lucky man to have a wife like her," Bapu said.

Mohan didn't answer. All he could think to talk about at the dinner was school. That was dull compared to the interesting things Kasturbai seemed to see everywhere. At last the meal was over. The sweets were passed and hands were washed. The scent of flowers was strong on the air. Night birds began singing. Mohan could not stop looking at Kasturbai. How could she have changed so much?

"Look, they are newlyweds again," Lakshmidas said. His wife shushed him quickly. At last, Mohan and Kasturbai were alone in their room. "I did miss you," she said. As they cuddled, Mohan remembered how much fun she was and how he had missed her.

In the morning, Mohan's bad mood was gone. He brushed his teeth downstairs and washed. Then he said his prayers at the shrine. He hurried into the big room and sat down on his mat by the central rug. A bowl of yogurt and plates of fresh flatbreads sat in front of him. "Namaste," Bapu said from his mat on the other side of the carpet. "I hope you slept well."

"Namaste," Mohan answered. He pretended not to see his father's grin. Kasturbai hurried out of the kitchen carrying a plate of sliced fresh fruit. She placed the plate on the rug and stopped to dip a fig into the yogurt. Then she fed it to Mohan. Before he could thank her, she was gone. Women's laughter pealed from the kitchen.

What had she told them? Mohan wondered. He watched as his mother and the Lakshmidas wives brought out more bowls of food. His brothers arrived for breakfast, and then Kasturbai came in. She sat down gracefully beside Mohan. He could smell her and feel her warmth.

"We will be going to the market today," Ba said to Bapu.

"All of you?" Bapu asked in mock surprise. He looked around at his wife and three more young wives. "Then by nightfall I will be a poor man." Gales of laughter followed this. The women protested. Bapu rolled his eyes and smacked his forehead. Kasturbai wiped tears of laughter from her cheeks.

Mohan watched the scene as if from another room. His wife had never laughed so hard at his jokes. Jealous thoughts crowded his mind. Today she would buy beautiful things: silks and rings, sweet perfumes and henna. Mohan knew he could never pay for any of it. Her thanks would all go to his father. There was nothing in this day for Mohan but school. Hours and hours sitting on the dusty floor studying dry facts. He'd have nothing to talk about tonight either. Nothing that would make his family laugh. Nothing to impress his own wife.

Kasturbai caught his hand. He almost jerked it back in surprise. "What is wrong, my husband?" she asked.

Her voice was so sweet that Mohan nearly told her. Instead, he sat tall and said, "Wife, I do not like the idea of you going to the market."

Now she pulled her hand free. "Women go

to the marketplace every day," she said. "I must go. Your mother invited me, herself."

Mohan realized he was breathing hard. "Very well," he said stiffly. "But after school we will talk about where you may go and when."

Kasturbai looked as if he had hit her. Mohan wanted to reach out to her, to pat her cheek and apologize. That would seem weak, he told himself. Instead, he rose to his feet. "I am going to school," he said loudly. And he did.

During the day he could not keep his mind on schoolwork. The scene from breakfast kept running again through his mind. Why, he wondered, *why* did he act like such a fool in front of his wife? He found himself making fists under his desk. She was *his*, he thought angrily. This should have been so easy.

After school every day Kasturbai told him funny stories about the market. She talked about the beautiful clothes she had seen and the sweets and treats she was offered by the merchants.

Mohan listened, trying not to feel bad for himself. School was school. He had to go. He needed an education to support his wife someday. He would need a job fit for someone in his caste and in his family. This was his dharma. The Vaishya all learned some skill or other. The Gandhis were all important people in their communities. They made a difference. But that was so far in the future!

For now he had to listen to his wife talk about her easy life. He had to hear her praise his father for being so kind and generous and wonderful. He had to wonder if he mattered to her at all.

One day, she came home full of life and energy, chirping like a happy bird. "I have been to a friend's house, Mohan," she said. "We played all morning in the sunshine. Then her brother came home." Mohan sat up. "We made him a meal. He sat and talked with us. What an interesting life he has!" Mohan's face felt hot. Hadn't this interesting brother seen the red dot on Kasturbai's forehead? Didn't he know she was married? How dare he!

"He is a trader and has been to many countries," Kasturbai went on. "Oh, the things he has seen!"

"Wife, I do not want you going to this friend's house again."

At his words, she fell silent.

"I do not want you to go to the market every day either," Mohan said. "I will tell you when you may go out and where. Otherwise I want you here, at home." Kasturbai seemed about to cry. "Oh, you may go out—when I have given permission."

Kasturbai was still quiet, but her eyes held rebellion.

"Do you understand me, wife?" he demanded.

She bowed her head.

"Good," he said. He got up and left the room.

The next months passed peacefully. Mohan went to school in the morning. Kasturbai greeted him every afternoon and listened to his tales of school. She was quiet at meals, as a wife should be. Once or twice she asked to go to her friend's. Mohan almost said yes. Then he remembered the wonderful brother and said no instead. He allowed her to go to the market with the women one day a week. He got to pick the day.

Life was good. His grades improved, Kasturbai was under control, and he had a pretty friend to cuddle with every night.

One morning a great leak opened in the roof of the school. Workmen arrived to fix it. They were so noisy that the teachers could not teach. They sent their classes home very early.

Mohan and his brother stood in front of the high school. Some friends joined them. "A day off!" one of them said. "Let us get some sweets to celebrate." The group wandered toward the marketplace. They were being loud and silly, but Mohan didn't mind. No one would ever know. He had told Kasturbai to stay home today.

The boys roamed the streets, laughing at the sellers and teasing the women who were shopping. "Ba, you don't want that cauliflower," one of the boys said. "It looks too much like your brother." They all laughed as the old woman clucked her tongue at them.

"You have eaten too many candies already," another boy said to a fat woman at the sweet booth. Mohan was ashamed but he laughed along with the boys.

"Move along!" a shopkeeper said. "Pests, all of you. A pack of dogs."

One boy made a barking sound. Soon all of them were barking like dogs and many heads turned to look.

Suddenly Karsandas was pulling on Mohan's sleeve. "Isn't that our Ba?" he asked. Mohan looked. It was his mother—and Kasturbai was there too. In the market. Without his permission. And he was barking like a dog.

Anger burst within Mohan. Had he no freedom to have fun? He stormed over to Kasturbai. "Follow me, wife. We're going home. Now." He turned on his heel and stalked away. As he left the tent he caught a glimpse of her. She was following him. He walked faster.

He was out of breath when they reached the Gandhi home. He was not out of anger. "What were you doing in the marketplace?" he demanded. "You had no right to be there!"

Kasturbai covered her face with her hands and ran to the woman's part of the house.

"Wait!" Mohan shouted. "Come back here!" But she was gone—and into a place he dared not go. Mohan paced back and forth in the front hall. She had to come out sometime, he thought. He practiced the lecture he would give her.

The words froze when the front door opened. Ba stood there, her face tight with anger. "Son," she said. "Follow me." Mohan felt like a little child as he trailed her into the shrine. She left a candy by the statue of Vishnu and knelt to pray. Mohan lit candles and knelt down too.

In the quiet, his anger melted into regret. His behavior in the marketplace had embarrassed his mother. Worse, it had earned him bad karma. He looked up at the pictures around the altar. There was one of Vishnu as a boy. A God who'd been a boy could understand. Mohan prayed to the boy-God.

Beside him he heard the silk of his mother's sari swishing. Her bracelets jingled too, as she rose. "Walk with me," she said softly. "There are things you should know." As they walked the halls of the Gandhi house, Ba told him that Kasturbai had been going to the marketplace almost daily. When she wasn't out shopping, she often went to friends' homes. "But she is a good wife," Ba said. "She is always at home, washed, calm, and ready to greet you as you wish."

"But I told her—" Mohan began. His mother cut him off.

"Kasturbai is not a toy. You cannot tuck her into your pocket when you are done playing with her." Mohan flinched. His mother was not done. "She is more like a plant who needs tending every day. She needs sun and air and room to grow—just like you do."

"A flowering plant," Mohan said. He liked the picture.

"But a woman is so much more," Ba said. "Kasturbai is full of strength and beauty. At the wedding, she promised to care for you for life and have your children. She also promised to be your friend—and you swore to be hers. It is time to keep your part of the bargain."

When Mohan began to speak, Ba put her fingers against his lips. She pointed at a door. Mohan was surprised to see that they had circled back to the shrine. He slipped in silently, knelt, and bowed his head. He had a lot to sort out, and Ba was right. Silence and prayer were the best places to think.

"You may go to the market whenever you like," Mohan told Kasturbai that night. "Please tell me when you are planning to visit a friend. That way I will know about your life as you know about mine."

* * * *

After school the next day Kasturbai was relaxed and joyful again. She chattered on and on about the market and told stories. Mohan could not help but smile. She was like a candle lit in a dark room, he thought—or a flower bursting into bloom.

"Wait," Mohan said. He took hold of her hands. "New bangle bracelets?" They jangled together on her slender wrists like little bells. "Ba wears them too. Why so many?"

"A woman's bracelets are supposed to give her husband a long life," Kasturbai said. She blushed.

Mohan sent a silent prayer of thanks to Vishnu and kissed his wife.

# CHAPTER 5

# TEMPTATION

Mohan could tell he was growing up. He was getting taller, although only a little. His beard had begun to grow, and the family had feasted the event. When Kasturbai had left for her parents' house again he was not so upset. She was pregnant now and would return in time to have their first baby.

Her absence gave him time to think about how much she had taught him. She had shown him how to get his own way without fighting. Kasturbai simply did not obey the silly rules he made for her. It made him see how wrong his rules were. Then he had to change them. Ba had approved. Kasturbai had not broken the rule of ahisma, nonviolence. She had worshipped the gods and gone to temple with Ba while Mohan was in school. She was a good woman. She was his wife.

Now that Mohan was fifteen, his mother looked like a little old lady to him. Ba still fasted to purify herself before religious holidays. She fasted to punish herself too. Mohan had never seen her do anything wrong. When he asked what she was punishing herself for, Ba said, "I am working to perfect myself from the inside."

Mohan had other goals. He was finally being accepted by the boys at school. His ring of friends grew. They didn't just like him because his father was Dewan, either. Mohan was funny. He was good at settling arguments. He seemed wise.

"It's because he spends so much time at the temple," Karsandas said of his brother. "Thinking. He is always thinking."

"Can our friend Sheik Mehtab come over for the afternoon?" Karsandas asked one day at dinner.

"I don't like him," Bapu said. "That boy always seems to be in trouble."

"He's the police chief's son," Mohan defended Sheik. "Maybe they are just harder on him."

"He can't eat here," Ba said. "He's a Muslim."

"I think it would be good for him to learn from me," Mohan said. "Perhaps I can show him how the Hindu religion is better."

"Show him the truth," Bapu said. "And stay true to yourself."

"Yes, yes, Bapu," Mohan said. His father was always talking about the truth. The point was that Mohan had friends now, important ones.

Sheik made it easy for Mohan to change him. He was always bringing up meat eating. This was Mohan's chance to turn Sheik against meat. They talked about it endlessly. Mohan made his best arguments. Somehow Sheik always had a better way to look at it.

"Have you seen the British?" Sheik asked Mohan one day. There was no need to answer that. British boys did not go to their school, but their parents lived in the finest houses in town. They ruled the whole country. Everyone had seen Englishmen.

"Have you ever wondered where they get their power?" Mohan had no answer for that. "They eat meat. It makes them grow tall. It makes them powerful. A few hundred of them control millions of Indians."

"No," Mohan said. "Meat isn't the answer." But he was trying to remember if he had ever seen a short Englishman. He shook his head. They all were taller than his own father. Even some Englishwomen were taller than Bapu.

"Look at me," Sheik said, standing up in the sunshine of the courtyard. Mohan had to gaze up at him. Sheik flexed the muscles in his arms and showed off his broad chest. "I am tall. I am strong. I am captain of three sports teams at the high school. And you are . . . ?"

It made Mohan think about how short he was. And how funny-looking. "So what?" he asked angrily.

Sheik ignored him. "This is because I Eat Meat." The words rang in the empty courtyard.

After that day, Sheik reminded him often about how he had made his point. And he dared Mohan to eat meat too. "Try it once," he said. "You will feel a difference right away."

Finally Mohan broke down. "Where would *I* get meat?" he challenged his friend. "I can't get it at my home. If I bought some in town, word would get back to Ba and Bapu. Besides, I promised to live according to Hindu laws."

"You promised to be small and weak? All to avoid one mouthful of meat?" Sheik laughed. His words stung.

"I have a plan," Sheik said the next day at school. "I will buy a piece of goat meat tomorrow and take it to the river outside of town. Come to meet me. You can watch me cook it. Then, if you don't want any, you can just leave. No one will ever know about it."

Mohan agreed. He would refuse the meat just as Ba refused to eat for days and days. He would show Sheik what true power was!

The next morning, the meat, cooking on a spit over a crackling fire, actually smelled good. Sheik used spices and brought warm crusty bread too. He made the food look so tasty that Mohan let himself try a little bite.

He swallowed it quickly, trying not to think about what it was—or what it meant. He had broken the rule against taking a life. He had eaten with a Muslim, too. Mohan closed his eyes.

Nothing happened.

The gods did not strike him dead. He did not feel a surge of power either.

"Well?" Sheik teased him. "Not bad, is it? Take another bite." Mohan did. The taste was strange; the feel of it in his mouth, even stranger. "Good for you!" Sheik congratulated him as he cut another piece. Together, they ate it all.

Afterward, Mohan's head was whirling. That could have been from the forbidden food or from the secrets Sheik told him by the cook fire. "Your brother Karsandas has eaten meat too," he said. "I have seen it. So has your older brother Lakshmidas."

Mohan had nightmares that night. He looked closely at his brothers the next morning. Nothing showed. He dared not ask them if what Sheik had said was true. He had sounded very sure.

At school the next day, Sheik invited him for another secret meal. "Yes," Mohan heard himself say. Again and again they met in the park to eat meat. Sometimes they were alone. Other times there were more boys along.

Once Ba sniffed at Mohan's skin. "You smell different," she said. "Do you feel well?" He told her he was fine. Then he bathed, scrubbing any meat scent away.

At school, Mohan watched Sheik befriend other young Hindu boys. It gave him a terrible idea. The next time he was alone with Sheik, he said, "You're not trying to get them to eat meat too?"

"What harm would that be?" Sheik answered calmly.

This was just a game to Sheik!

Mohan decided never to speak with him again—or to eat any more meat.

"What happened to your Muslim friend?" Bapu asked at dinner. He looked ill.

"We are no longer friends," Mohan admitted. "You were right about him. He was just trouble. Besides, I have other friends." And he would say no more.

Those other friends smoked. Though Mohan knew his family would object, he began smoking too. It felt deliciously wicked to Mohan. He told himself it was not a sin like eating meat. But paying for cigarettes was a problem. None of the boys had any money. They had to steal the cigarettes. Or sometimes they just stole coins to buy them. That *was* a sin, and Mohan knew it. He was gathering bad karma. But it was like a game, too—a game all of his friends had fun playing.

It made him feel grown up to do something on his own like this; something that would make his parents mad.

Next, his gang decided they should seek out women in the city. "I can't," Mohan said as they laughed at him. "I vowed at my wedding never to be intimate with anyone but Kasturbai." They teased him for being afraid of his wife. They said he was a coward. They said he was no man if he did not do this.

All the while, Mohan thought. Kasturbai had been gone for months. He really missed her. He was lonely. Perhaps it would be like the meat or the cigarettes and stealing. It wouldn't matter if no one found out.

"I'll go," he said.

They all agreed on a time and place. Mohan met them there. But the wrongness of it overwhelmed him. He turned and ran out.

Home had never smelled so good to him. He rushed into the household shrine and lit all the candles. He offered the gods every bit of money left in his pockets, and then fell to his knees. What had he done? And why?

It was over, he told himself. All of it. He vowed never to be so weak again—so weak that he would fall for temptations. Now he would pick his friends more carefully. He would—what had his father said to him?—"stay true to himself." His stomach knotted up. *Lies,* he thought. His life had become lies and theft and sins. All night long he tried to think of how he could make up for the way he'd been living.

"Mohan?" He looked up at the sound of his mother's soft voice. "I'm so sorry to interrupt. Have you seen your father?" He was unwell at dawn, she told him. Bapu had gone for a walk and hadn't returned.

Mohan found his father. He was not out-doors at all. Instead, right in the middle of the morning, he had gone back to bed. Bapu had not felt well for weeks. Now he was clearly sick.

"Ba!" Mohan cried. His mother hurried in and medicines were ordered. Mr. Gandhi did not seem to get better. He did not seem to get worse either, though he stopped presiding at family meals. Mostly he stayed in bed.

Back at school, Mohan kept to himself. The

rowdy crowd left him alone. Sheik never came to talk to him. He had a new young friend. "I do not need any of them," Mohan told himself. Besides, he had fallen behind in his studies again. He needed the time to catch up.

Most of all, he had to become strong inside. His mother was strong. Ba could turn away from her own hunger and go without food for days at a time. Mohan wished he had turned away from his friends when they'd tempted him. Perhaps, Mohan thought, he could build inner strength by refusing things he wanted. There were many easy things he could do without. He loved sweets. Could he turn away from them for a week? He tried, and found he was strong enough for that.

Could he do without food for a day? That was hard. The rest of the family ate regular meals, but Mohan resisted. It felt good to prove that his inner strength was growing.

He was always tempted by the sound of birds outside and street noises. Could he force himself to focus on schoolwork and not daydream? That took a lot of strength. It too, became easier as he practiced.

But that did not erase all the bad karma he had gathered in his weakness. It haunted him.

"Mohan!" Ba waved a letter at him when he came home from school one day. "Kasturbai is coming back! She will be here in a week!"

When his wife arrived, Mohan could not help but stare at her belly. It was so round! "Will you explode?" he asked. She only laughed at him. So did the women gathered around to greet her. "May I touch it?" he asked. Ba hissed in disapproval, but Kasturbai guided his hand to the biggest part of her bulge. "It is hard!" he cried. He got silent for a few moments gazing at Kasturbai's face. Suddenly he shouted, "I can feel it! Our baby. He is in there!"

The women laughed again, but it was kind laughter. Mohan joined in.

Expecting a baby made everything worse. Mohan wanted to be a father like Bapu. But

Bapu was honest. Bapu told the truth. Mohan's sins dragged him down as he walked around. Sitting next to sweet Kasturbai he only felt unworthy. Passing a dinner plate to his saintly mother, Mohan felt dirtied by his secrets. Everyone he looked at in the high school seemed to know how far he had fallen—even the teachers. Only his dear, sick Bapu did not know.

It took more praying and more thinking before Mohan decided how to solve this problem. He could not talk with Kasturbai about it. When she begged him to tell her what was wrong, he always said "nothing."

Ba even asked if he would like to talk to the Brahmin family friend. "He is a good priest, you know, and wise."

But Mohan was working on a confession. He wanted to share it with his father, who valued truth above all. He wrote down all of his sinful behavior except for eating meat. That was far too awful to tell Ba. At the end of the list, Mohan said he had learned his lesson. He promised to be stronger now. Then he begged his father for forgiveness. If Bapu could forgive him, Mohan could forgive himself. He just had to find the right time to give it to Bapu.

It took weeks to build up the courage. One evening he wandered into his father's bedroom. Mohan knelt by the sleeping mat. "Bapu," he said quietly. His father opened his eyes. "I want you to know the truth." He watched his own hand tremble as he reached over to give him the paper. Then Mohan sat back and closed his eyes. He could barely breathe, waiting for Bapu's reaction.

There was no sound at all. Then there was a sigh. Mohan opened his eyes. Bapu was looking right at him. His face was sad, but it was full of love. And there were tears running down his cheeks. But his eyes still held love.

Mohan bowed to him silently and left.

"I'll take over caring for Bapu," Mohan told his mother. "My uncle has done a fine job, but he is old, too. I am young. I have more energy.

And I want to be close to Bapu now."

Ba agreed. For weeks, Mohan kept cool wet cloths on his father's face. He wiped Bapu's body when it was drenched in sweat. He changed the sheets and kept the curtains closed so the light would not hurt his father's eyes.

It was hard work and the hours were long. Few people would come into the room. The job was lonely and frightening. As his father got worse, Mohan longed for company. He wanted a hug. In the dark sickroom, Mohan knew exactly what he needed: Kasturbai.

He called for his uncle and begged a few hours off. When it was arranged, Mohan hurried to his own bedroom. Kasturbai was asleep. She made a big lump in the bed now. "Wake up," Mohan pleaded. "I need to talk. I need a hug. I am so tired."

Kasturbai turned and sat up. She stretched out her arms, and Mohan nestled close to her. Presently he fell asleep in her arms.

They awoke to a pounding on the door.

"Get up!" The voice was Kasandar's. The news was terrible. "Come at once. Bapu has died!"

The next days passed in a blur. The friends. The ceremonies. The burning of Bapu's body. "Did he call to God in his last moments?" everyone asked. "If he said, *'Hey, Ram,'* 'Oh, God,' as he died, he will be welcomed by Vishnu himself. He might even get to stop his endless cycle of lives." Mohan had to say he didn't know. He wasn't there when Bapu died. It all felt unreal. Then they were back in the house. They had to eat even though no one was hungry. Voices were hushed. Curtains were closed. The only good thing, everyone agreed, was the baby who would come soon. Kasturbai and Mohan as new parents? A new little life? That was what the household needed.

Lakshmidas went back to work. Karsandas left school and found a job to make some money for the family. Mohan had to go back to high school. He had a year and a half left before graduating. "Can't I quit and take a job like

Lakshmidas? Or like Karsandas?" he begged. "I want to help the family."

When he would not listen to Ba or his uncle, they called the Brahmin priest, Joshi, in to talk with him.

"One of you Gandhi children must prepare to be the next dewan," the wise man told him. "The prince only wants educated people around him. You are the youngest son but you are the brightest." Joshi rested his hands on Mohan's shoulders and looked straight into his eyes. "You must go to college, Mohandas. You must become a lawyer."

"A lawyer! That means more years of schooling!"

"I will help," said the Brahmin. "Mohandas, this is your dharma. You must do your duty to your family. You have grown up in the last months. You are ready to do this now."

Mohan bowed his head. The priest was right.

Within days, Kasturbai had the baby.

Everyone gathered to see the new mother

and her child. They all cooed, "How beautiful!" and "She is perfect." "A new Gandhi!" and "A blessing!"

But when Kasturbai could not hear, they said other things. "The child is so weak!" "She does not cry for food!" "Why doesn't that baby squirm and wiggle? Something is very wrong with her."

Mohan could tell the baby was ill when he held her in his arms. Kasturbai feared the worst. "What if she dies?" she wailed to her husband.

"It is in the hands of the gods," Mohan said. His eyes filled with tears. "Her soul will just come back in another body, you know."

"Why did she have to leave our family?" Kasturbai wailed when the baby died. "Are the gods punishing *us*?"

Mohan had a terrible thought: What if his weakness was to blame? He had turned to Kasturbai for comfort when Bapu was dying. "I don't think so," he lied.

"At sixteen, you are both young," Ba said, after the baby had been set adrift in the river. "There will be other children. You still have years to give me grandsons and granddaughters. Just you wait." There was such joy in her voice that Kasturbai smiled a little. Even Mohan relaxed.

The family grieved the death of Bapu and of the little nameless one. The house was full of sadness. Mohan plunged back into school-work. He had a goal now: his dharma to become a lawyer. Kasturbai clung to him.

Soon she had an announcement for the family. "Mohan and I will be having another baby," she said. When everyone began to congratulate them, Kasturbai held up her hand. "I will not believe this until I hear him cry like a healthy baby."

She left soon after this to spend months with her old family. Mohan's grades rose. He entered his last year in high school. He kept exercising his willpower and studying his religion.

Kasturbai returned in a few months. The household waited to see if she could have a healthy child. They did not even celebrate at the childbirth.

"It is a son," Ba told Mohan.

"And . . . ?" Mohan asked, before he even asked to see the child. "And he seems very healthy," his mother said with a smile.

Soon the house was full of the baby's lusty cries. He ate and wiggled and grabbed at fingers. "Little Harilal is fine," the priest said. "Kasturbai is a wonderful mother. They will both thrive now."

They did. Harilal was just walking when Mohan went to a college three hours away from home.

Mohan was miserable. He missed Kasturbai. He missed Ba, too. And he could not understand all of the professor's words. Mohan could read English easily. Spoken English was much harder for him. Mohan was tired of the struggle.

"You aren't thinking of dropping out of school, are you?" Joshi asked. It was vacation time. A family conference had been called. All of the uncles and brothers sat in a circle on cushions and mats, talking about Mohan's future.

"He can't drop out!" an uncle said.

"Our father had no college degree, but times have changed," Lakshmidas said. "You need a degree now. You need good English. Englishmen run the courts and the country. You have to be able to deal with them."

"May I speak?" Mohan asked. When the uncles quieted down, Mohan said, "I have been thinking I would like to be a doctor."

"No!" the calls came from all around. "Hindus must never touch dead flesh." "Doctors study dead bodies." "You can't study medicine!" "You *must* be a lawyer!" Mohan slumped lower and lower.

Joshi's calm voice broke through the chaos. "Mohan, I have an idea." Mohan sat up again.

"Yes, you should be a lawyer. But you don't have to get your degree in India. To be powerful in the courts the Englishmen have set up here, you should get a degree from England."

Mohan was stunned. Go to England? He'd be right in the middle of their power. His inner strength had grown and now he could add English power to it!

"You'd be there for three years, with everyone around you speaking English. . . . Mohan, are you listening?" Joshi's voice broke into Mohan's thoughts.

"Yes, I will go!" Mohan said, to everyone's surprise. "Can we afford it? We could sell Kasturbai's jewelry. I could work for a year. I must do this!"

Kasturbai agreed to sell her jewels, but Lakshmidas told her not to. "I'll pay for the trip," he said. "It is an investment in the family."

Ba did not want her youngest son to go so far away. "You must promise me three things if you wish to leave," she told her son. "There will be many temptations in England. You must swear not to drink alcohol, not to eat meat, and to stay faithful to Kasturbai."

Mohan made these solemn promises, and Ba gave him her blessing.

After weeks of planning and packing and paperwork for the government, it was time to go. Mohan said good-bye to his wife and son. His brothers, their wives, his uncles and their wives plus their children all came to wave good-bye. Ba came too, of course. "Remember your oaths!" she said.

Mohan heard an echo of his father's words: *Stay true to yourself.*

"I will," he promised, and boarded the train to Bombay, where he expected to catch the boat to England.

"Mohandas K. Gandhi, you cannot go to England," he was told by the leader of his Vaishya caste. "It will ruin your standing as a Hindu."

Mohan thought quickly. This rule was unfair. Kasturbai would just ignore it. He tried to think what an Englishman would do. What was the truth of this?

"This is none of your business, good sirs," he said. "I do this for family."

"Then you will be an outcaste forever," the Vaishya leader said. "Anyone who comes to the dock to wave good-bye to you will be fined!"

Mohan turned and walked toward the boat, his head held high.

## CHAPTER 6
# THE ENGLISHMAN

Mohan was eighteen in 1888 when he boarded the steamship bound for London. He felt ready to meet any challenge.

That did not last long.

The English sailors spoke fast and had so many different accents, it was almost impossible for him to understand what they were saying. It was even worse with the other passengers. In the dining room plates were set up on tables, not on the floor. There were chairs to sit on, not cushions. And everyone was eating with strange metal tools instead of with their fingers. Mohan only glanced at the food. Which recipes had meat in them and which didn't? He didn't know—and he couldn't ask.

Mohan went back to his cabin. He got some ship's food brought to him over the next three weeks. Mostly he lived on the sweets and fruit he had brought with him.

He stepped out only when he saw someone who might speak his language. That way he met two men who offered to help get him settled in London. They showed him how to use a fork and a knife. They told him what food to avoid. They laughed when they saw the white summer-weight suit he was saving for his arrival in London.

He walked off the boat into a cool, foggy September day and shivered. All the other men on the dock were dressed in warm black jackets. Mohan's new friends laughed again. "Nobody really cares what you wear," they told him.

But Mohan did. He was led to a hotel. Even the man who carried his suitcases was dressed in fancy clothes with gold buttons and braid all over his black jacket. "He is only a *bellhop*," one friend explained. "He's a servant, not some important official." The friends helped Mohan register, and then rushed with him into a little closet. Doors slid closed behind them. To Mohan's great surprise, the closet suddenly jerked upward. He gasped. Both of his new friends laughed loudly.

"This is an *elevator*," they explained. "We use it instead of stairs." The friends walked Mohan to his new room and went on to their own homes.

Gandhi ignored the chair. He walked past the bed. Instead, he sat right down on the floor, overwhelmed. Everything here was so different! He rose to answer a knock at his door. The bellhop stood outside with a cart carrying all of his suitcases.

"Namaste," Mohan said politely, folding his hands and bowing slightly.

"I don't know about all that," the bellhop said. "Do you want help with your suitcases or not?"

Mohan stood aside, and the man hustled his things into the room. When he was done, the bellhop stood with a hand extended.

"Namaste," Mohan said again. The bellhop didn't move. Mohan remembered seeing Englishmen shake hands. He grabbed the bellhop's hand with his and pumped it up and down.

The bellhop rolled his eyes and pulled away. "Dirty foreigner," he grumbled. "Cheapskate." He had been waiting for a tip.

Mohan shut the door behind him and took a deep breath.

In the next few weeks, Mohan scurried about the city, trying not to attract attention. He found a cheaper room in a boardinghouse. He found his school, The Inns of Court, and registered for classes. He watched the Englishmen all around him. The true gentlemen were the ones who got respect.

Gandhi decided to be an English gentleman. He spent a lot of his money on handsome black suits and a top hat. Gentlemen wore gloves, too. He bought himself a pair made of soft leather and a pair of leather shoes. At least, he told himself, he wasn't *eating* the animals whose skin he was wearing. He grew a great bushy mustache too. Finally he bought a silver-topped cane. Mohan signed himself up for dancing lessons and tried to learn the violin, too. He took a class in the proper way to speak English. Now when he walked the streets, he felt like he fit right in.

But one day he caught sight of himself in a mirror. He looked strange. He did not look English—but he did not look Indian, either. *Be true to yourself,* Bapu always said.

"I am Mohandas K. Gandhi," he told himself. "I am an Indian becoming a lawyer." Mohan decided to give up all his silly lessons. They were expensive and took time away from his studies. He could become the best possible lawyer—but he could not become an Englishman. He was Indian. This was *a Truth.* Mohan breathed a sigh of relief.

Surrounded by people speaking English, Mohan learned fast. Within a week, the professors seemed to be speaking much more clearly.

Mohan had less trouble talking with classmates. A month passed, and Mohan could not remember ever having struggled with the language.

He had a hard time finding food to eat. The dining room at the school, the boardinghouse, and local restaurants all served meat at every meal. Everything seemed to be covered in meat gravy, or sitting in meat sauces, fried in animal fat, or cooked right in with meat. "Oh, relax," his classmates teased at him. "Why don't you just eat like us while you are here? You can always go back to being a vegetarian when you go home."

Mohan refused. He was a Hindu. Besides, he had made a promise to his mother. He loved her. He missed her. And he thought about her as he walked hungry miles around the city looking for food. If she could control her hunger, he could too. At last, he found a few vegetarian restaurants. He began to eat in them regularly. Mohan began to notice others who came to the same restaurants. Gradually he made new friends there.

Someone told him to read *A Plea for Vege-tarianism*. The arguments in the book made him think differently. Now his mother wasn't the only thing making him avoid meat. He had come to see that it was not only cheaper and healthier to be a vegetarian, but spiritually bet-ter for him too.

One day Mohan saw a poster inviting every-one to a meeting of the London Vegetarian Society. Mohan went, out of curiosity. The room was filled with men and a few women. Unlike his new friends from school, these were people of all ages. As they introduced them-selves, Mohan was impressed.

These were important people in London: scholars, intellectuals, and radical thinkers. They believed in nonviolence even though they'd never heard of ahisma. "We try to live simple lives," they explained. They had cut out extras to leave themselves energy for deep thought. Mohan had already tried that on his own. Now he was surrounded with people who used their inner strength. Mohan gave up all spices. He didn't need them—though he did love the tastes of curry and cinnamon. Mohan was learning in classes. Now he was eager to learn all this group could teach him too.

"I am Sir Edwin Arnold," one elegantly dressed man said. "I am so glad we have a Hindu member now. I translated your ancient holy book, into English. I would love to talk to you about it."

"Well, sir, I have not actually read it myself." Mohan was embarrassed.

"Take my copy, young man," Sir Edwin urged. "Let me know when you are done."

Mohan took the precious book back to his room. "The *Song of God*," he whispered its English title before he opened it. He had always known it held the basic principles of Hindu philosophy. That sounded dull and the book was large, but the words, the thoughts, the beauty of it drew him in. Suddenly things were making sense to him. It all came together: right and wrong, the gods and goddesses, the history of India, and the nature of life. He skipped meals. He skipped classes. He read and reread parts of the *Bhagavad Gita* he didn't quite understand.

He had never thought more deeply. It felt wonderful.

He raced to the next meeting of the London Vegetarian Society and handed the book back to Sir Edwin. "There is no need for thanks," the man said. "I can see the excitement on your face. I have awakened your intellect! Shall we meet together for lunch and discuss what you think the *Gita* means?

It was the first of many long talks Mohan had with his adult friends about philosophy. When they had covered the entire *Bhagavad Gita,* another member of the Society asked, "Have you ever studied the Christian Bible?" He was not surprised when Mohan said no— but he had a copy ready for Mohan to study.

Their talks went on and on through the year. They discussed favorite passages. "I love the Sermon on the Mount," Mohan admitted. "'. . . whosoever shall smite thee on thy right cheek, turn to him the other, also. . . . and if any man . . . take away thy coat, let him have thy cloak also,'" he quoted. "That makes me shiver, it is so beautiful."

He looked around quickly, but in this room of thinkers, no one laughed.

He went on reciting: "'Love your enemies, bless them that curse you, do good to them that hate you, and pray for them which despitefully use you and persecute you.'" All around him, men were nodding as they thought about the difficult teaching.

"Have you read about the Buddha?" another Society member asked. He too had a book to loan Mohan and time to discuss the ideas of Buddhism. Over the next year, Mohan studied Mohammed's life too, and his teachings. The more he read, the more he thought. The more he learned, the more peaceful he felt inside. All the beautiful truths seemed to him to fit together.

Mohan was learning about English law, too. That took another kind of thinking. And there was a beauty in the government, too. It was designed to give people freedom but keep them safe. Democracy. Justice for all. Equality. These fine ideas were as deep and profound as anything from his religious studies.

Mohan and his classmates argued the laws in class. Then they discussed them over steaming cups of tea. The professors held special meetings to talk about difficult points of law with their students. Sometimes Mohan's mind felt exhausted by all the thinking—but it felt good. In the end, he decided that English Common Law might be complex and fussy in the details, but at its heart was a beautiful ideal.

Mohan passed his bar exam on June 10, 1891. That meant he was a lawyer. He couldn't wait to get home and hug Kasturbai. It had been three years since he had seen her! And Ba—what wonderful talks he could have with her now. He understood so much more about religion and how to be a truly good person, like her. Two days after graduation he was on a ship headed back to India.

## CHAPTER 7
# PREJUDICE

"Namaste, Lakshmidas!" Mohan yelled the moment he saw his brother at the dock. "Namaste!" He pushed his way down the gangplank and began to run toward Lakshmidas. The closer he got, the worse Lakshmidas looked.

"What is it?" Instead of hugging his brother, he asked, "What is wrong?"

Tears dripped down Lakshmidas's face before he could get the words out. "Mohan, little Mohan, Ba has died."

"Mother? When?" Mohan demanded.

"A few days ago. She tried to wait for you. . . ." Lakshmidas could say no more. Numb with sorrow, Mohan followed him to the train and home.

Kasturbai greeted him in the courtyard. She was holding a little boy's hand. "Harilal," she said, pulling him toward Mohan. "This is your father." The boy hung back until Mohan handed him sweets he had bought on the way home.

Harilal bowed until his head touched Mohan's feet. "You are a nice man," the boy said. "Ba told me. I am four now." He held up four fingers.

"You must call him 'Bapu,'" Kasturbai said. Her face was beautiful now, Mohan thought. She was finally a grown woman. And her eyes! She looked at him and he could not look away.

"Bapu," Harilal said. "Old Ba is gone to her next life. No one wants to play here anymore."

"I will play soon, son," Mohan said, still looking at Kasturbai. "I too am very, very sad. Ba was a saint, you know."

Harilal looked at his mother. She nodded to the child. "Old Ba was your Bapu's own mother. Bapu might not feel like playing just yet."

"Yes, Ba," Harilal said. He turned and

skipped back into the house. When Mohan entered with Kasturbai on his arm, the old house seemed different. "We have sold some chests and books," she explained. "We let some servants go, too. And without old Ba, now . . ." Her lips quivered as she struggled to stay in control. "It does seem very empty here." She gave a ragged sigh. "At least you are home, my husband." The bracelets on her wrists jingled as she patted his arm.

Hearing how little money the family had left, Mohan began at once looking for a job in Rajkot. There were none. Even their Brahmin friend, Joshi, could find no work for him. Now that Mohan had lived in the huge city of London, Rajkot seemed like a sad little place to live, anyhow.

He wrote some letters and got a job in Bombay. The city was big and busy. After London, though, it seemed dirty and poor to Mohan. He moved Kasturbai and Harilal to an apartment there and reported to work.

The company was happy to have a London-educated lawyer. They gave him an important case to argue in court. Mohan went right to work, talking to the man accused of a crime. He never raised his voice. Instead, he asked the man quiet, thoughtful questions. He listened carefully and thought a long time before asking the next question. In that way, he leaned more than enough to prove his client innocent.

Mohan wrote out what he would say to the judge. He forgot about the jury. He also forgot about the other lawyer—the one he would be arguing against.

When the court day came, Mohan knew exactly how things were supposed to happen. A courtroom, he thought, was a quiet, calm place where everyone wanted the same wonderful things: Freedom. Security. Democracy. Justice for all. Equality.

It was not like that at all. The other lawyer was an Englishman. He spoke so loudly, he was almost yelling. Mohan's voice was soft and thoughtful. The other lawyer was quick with his words and quicker with his mind. He winked at the English judge and strutted like a peacock. The crowd in the courtroom laughed at his jokes. Some of the cruel things he said were so clever, they laughed at them, too.

Mohan had practiced what he wanted to say, but the arguments didn't fit now. Not against this man. He tried to think of answers that were clever and kind and true, too. It took so long for him to find the right words that someone in the crowd giggled. "Speak up, Mr. Gandhi," the judge demanded. All of Mohan's childhood memories of bullies came back at him. His old shyness took over. He felt his face flush. His voice sounded strangled now, and his words came out jumbled.

The second time Mohan had to pause to think, the crowd laughed—not because he was clever, but because he was slow. They couldn't know that his brilliant mind needed time to consider points of law that even the judge never thought of. All they saw was a fool—one pretending to be a fancy London lawyer.

It was a disaster. Gandhi went back to the office and quit before he could be fired. Now he *really* needed a job. He could not get another one in Bombay. Not after that trial. He moved his wife and son back to little Rajkot.

Lakshmidas got him a new job as a law secretary. Mohan felt awful. Lakshmidas was the one who had paid for his law degree. On a secretary's salary he could not hope to pay his brother back. Mohan still had to support Kasturbai and Harilal. And now his wife was expecting another child. Mohan felt desperate.

"Little brother," Lakshmidas said one day, "didn't you tell me you got to know the British agent named Charles Ollivant while you were in London?"

"We spoke once or twice," Mohan said cautiously. The English were only fairly friendly to Indians in England. "Why?"

"I need you to talk to your friend." Here, Mohan winced. "I lost my job in Porbandar because of a lie someone told about me.

Ollivant is in power here now. He could get me my job back. You could talk him into it."

"Why don't you just use the justice system?" Mohan asked. "If you were wronged, the court of law would make it right."

Lakshmidas laughed out loud at him. "Where do you think we are? This is India. The English here take care of the English. If an Indian wants justice, he has to ask favors or pay bribes or make threats. Sometimes all three. And even then the law isn't fair with him. Please go. You do owe me this."

Mohan reluctantly went to see Agent Ollivant in the British offices. "Who are you?" the man asked, staring at him coldly.

"We met in London. You must remember." The Englishman rose to his feet and glared down at Mohan. "At the college?" He heard his voice growing smaller.

Mohan had heard that Englishmen treated Indians differently in India than they did in England. He had not believed it—until now.

Mr. Ollivant had been pleasant in London. He had made jokes. "Pardon me, Mr. Ollivant," he began.

"*Sahib*," the Englishman used the word that almost meant "master." "You call me *Sahib* Ollivant here."

"Well, then." Mohan avoided using the word hated by all Indians. "My brother was falsely accused when he worked for the prince of Rajkot. He wants his job back. You should look into the doings of your agent in that town."

"It is your sneaky brother who is the problem. Let him go to the courts himself if he thinks he could get justice. Now get out of here."

"Please let me finish," Mohan began. "There is more."

"Guard!" the Englishman called angrily. "Guard! Throw this foolish little man out." A tall English policeman stalked over to Mohan and grabbed him by the arm.

"Come along, you," he said, though he gave Mohan no time to get his feet under him. The guard dragged Mohan out through the door and down the hall. Then he actually threw him out the door. Mohan landed on his hands and knees on the dusty street. The guard stood looking at him calmly while he patted imaginary dirt off his hands.

*"Never,"* Mohan stormed at Lakshmidas, "never in my life have I been so humiliated! In the *street*. He threw me into the street like an Untouchable. I will sue him in court for this."

Lakshmidas smiled sadly and shook his head. "I almost expected as much," he said. "You will come to expect this treatment here, too."

"NO!" Mohan shouted. He calmed himself and said, "I will never accept this." But everywhere he looked in Rajkot, Mohan saw examples of the same thing. The English might talk about equality. But they treated Indians like dirt. India should be where *Indians* were in charge, Mohan thought angrily. The anger burned like a fire inside of him—but he had to keep it inside.

This new emotion joined the shame of his failure in court and the poverty of his little family. It was almost too much to bear.

Then Kasturbai had her baby. It was a son and it was healthy. They named him Manilal. The new baby brought some joy into Mohan's depression. But it also made getting a good job even more important.

Mohan decided to open a law office in Rajkot. But before he could start, he learned that Charles Ollivant had become the political officer of the area. Any court cases he did would be under Ollivant's control. Mohan knew that *Sahib* Ollivant would remember being upset by Mohandas K. Gandhi. And Mohan could never forget being treated like a worthless dog instead of as a London-trained lawyer of the proud Vaishya caste.

"Send Ollivant a letter apologizing for your

behavior," Lakshmidas said. "Better yet, send a letter and a box of fine cigars. You can get back on his good side." He looked at his little brother's face. "I'm sorry, Mohan. That is the way it works in India now."

"Not for me, it isn't!" Mohan said angrily. "I will never apologize when it is *I* who have been treated wrongly. Sahib Ollivant should apologize to *me*!"

"You will never get anywhere in British India with that attitude, little brother," Lakshmidas said.

Mohan knew now he was right. But he hated it. He was miserable at his secretary's job, but he kept working. His little family was growing up. Presently Kasturbai made a happy announcement. "Mohan, we are going to have a third child!" Now the need for more money was getting desperate.

The answer came from Lakshmidas. He had heard of a lawsuit between some people in India and others in South Africa. They had plenty of lawyers here, but needed one in

South Africa for a year. The pay was good. "You should take it, little brother," Lakshmidas said. "You are so unhappy here. A year away from India will do you good."

Mohan thought about it. The English ruled South Africa, too. He knew English law. Many, many Indians had moved to South Africa. He could find friends there and vegetarian food. There were Hindu temples he could go to. It would only mean a year away from his family. And he *really* needed the money. The decision was made.

In April of 1893, twenty-three-year-old Mohan left Bombay on a ship headed for South Africa.

When he arrived, he wore a turban on his head and a good suit to meet his new law partners. "Namaste. I am Abdullah Sheth," a turbaned man greeted him. "We will be working together." Over the next few weeks, Abdullah had to tell Mohan some hard truths about living in South Africa.

"There are many rules for life here," he

said. "Some of them are English Common Laws. You already know those. But there are other things you must know if you are going to be a success here."

He explained what Mohan had already seen in the streets. The black people were all treated like untouchables, even though Africa was their own land. More than three quarters of South Africans were Black, but they had no rights. The white people—the English and the Dutch—had total control.

"Like in India?" Mohan said bitterly.

"It is more complicated here," Abdullah said. He described another class of people—called "browns" or "coloreds"—who sat somewhere in the middle. "All Indians are considered brown," Abdullah went on. "Most of the Indians who were brought to South Africa are Untouchables. They are used for cheap labor. Upper-caste Indian families moved here too, but the English paid no attention to that. They treat all Indians the same—and bad. United, we might be able to do something about it. But all the Indian groups do here is fight among each other."

"Is that all?" Mohan asked. He told himself things could not be as bad as Abdullah was telling him.

"There are so many rules," Abdullah said. "More than I have time to list. I'm sure you will find out about them this year." He told Mohan it would take three long train rides and two bus rides to get to Pretoria, where he would be working. "You had better get on your way." They bowed to each other and then Abdullah said, "Oh, first, take off your turban." Mohan stared at the turban that Abdullah was wearing. He waited for an explanation. "Another rule." Abdullah shrugged. "Indians like me who are Arabs and Muslim are allowed to wear a turban. Other Indians are not." His face looked grim.

Mohan took off his turban. He bought a first-class ticket for the long, long trip and got on the train. Mohandas walked down the aisle and sat down in an empty compartment. No one joined him, though the train was filling up. Several stops later, Mohan looked out the window at the wide-open plains of the Transvaal. The Dutch ruled this part of South Africa. The sun set on low hills in the distance. Mohan dozed, barely noticing when the train stopped again.

"What is *this*?" An outraged voice woke him up. Before he could reply, the white man had gone down the aisle. Mohan rubbed his eyes.

Before the train left the lonely station on the plains, the man stormed back into the compartment. He was followed by a conductor. "You must go back to the third-class compartment," the train official said.

"But"—Mohan fumbled to find his ticket—"you can see I have a first-class ticket."

"Colored people are not allowed in this compartment," the official said coldly. "Now get out." The Englishman stared at Mohan and cleared his throat.

Mohan refused. He had the ticket. "I am Mohandas K. Gandhi," Mohan argued. "I am just as good as anyone else—as that Englishman, there!" He was still arguing when the conductor grabbed him by the arm and dragged him out of his seat. He pushed Mohan through the door just as the train whistle blew.

Mohan fell to the station platform. Before he could pick himself up, the conductor was locking his suitcases into a closet in the station. The train was leaving. It was nine o'clock at night. In a blind fury Mohan stared down the tracks. How dare they! He trembled with rage. His fists clenched and unclenched. He kicked a stone out into the darkness.

*Ahisma.* Nonviolence. His rage quieted when he realized he was losing control.

He shivered in the cold air and looked around. No shops or homes clustered near the county station. One road ran past. It disappeared into darkness in both directions. Mohan pulled his thin coat around him. His overcoat was back on the train along with his luggage. It would be the hottest part of the year at home, he thought. Here in the southern hemisphere, it was the coldest. He watched his breath steam in the air.

What would he do?

There had to be another train coming along. He looked at a chart on the wall. There was one in the morning. He would catch that. Mohan settled down against the wall of the empty station. He wrapped his arms around his chest and tucked his hands into the warmth of his armpits. He waited. The anger grew again inside of him.

The wait would be long. Twelve hours. It would be cold. There was nothing he could do now but think. And Mohan had a lot to think about.

Should he stay in South Africa? He had a job here. It would be hard to go home to Kasturbai after failing again. It would be even worse to go home to Lakshmidas. But here he could be treated like an Untouchable anytime he broke the rules. If he wanted to work here, he would have to make nice to the despised

Englishmen. He had too much pride for that. He was a *Gandhi*!

He thought of his father. Mohan had hours to wait, so he tried to remember all that his father had taught him. Then he thought of his dear Ba. What would she want him to do? He thought of Joshi and all the advice he had given over the years.

Mohan reviewed the English laws he had studied in London. There were many that should help him now ... and not here when his skin was brown. The beautiful English ideal of equality under the law did not apply to him. This was so unfair!

Should he go home to India? His family was there. It was his country, after all. But he could be thrown into the street there, too. If he wanted to work he would have to make nice to the despised Englishmen in India for the rest of his life. He had too much pride for that. He was a *Gandhi*! It was time he started acting like one.

His stomach told him he was hungry. He

told it to be quiet. His body told him it was freezing cold. He made himself think of other things.

There were hours left in the night to think over his problem from all angles. That was what his lawyer training had taught him to do. And the years of deep thinking about many religions gave him wisdom to draw upon. As the night went on, he went deeper and deeper into thought.

He decided that he could not stand a life where people were so unfair to him. But what could he do about it? He could not change his color. He did not want to. He was Gandhi, an Indian, brown-skinned and proud of his heritage.

A new idea began to grow. One change he *could* make was in how people thought. That was what lawyers did all the time. The whites in South Africa were prejudiced against Indians. But the Indians of South Africa seemed prejudiced, too. Sixty-six thousand Indians just obeyed English rules without a struggle. They seemed to believe they were helpless. This was a great wrong, and Gandhi knew it. He could try to change their minds.

Gandhi was filled with hope for the first time since he'd left London. What a grand idea. Fighting prejudice. This could be his life's work!

He had to support his family, of course. He had to eat and bathe and keep his body healthy. But other than that, his path was clear. Before the sun rose at dawn, Gandhi made a vow to himself. For his next year in Africa, he would use all his strength and training to win freedom for Indians!

CHAPTER 8
# THE FIGHT BEGINS

Gandhi caught the next train to Pretoria, then the stagecoaches. On one coach, he was told to ride outside on the ledge where the driver's feet rested. On another stagecoach Gandhi was surprised when an Englishman defended him. Perhaps not all the whites were so prejudiced, he thought.

Finally, Gandhi found himself a room in a boardinghouse in Pretoria. He needed to collect information there about a case for his law firm. He went right to work with a new energy. He couldn't wait to get to his real purpose in South Africa, fighting prejudice.

He read the papers and talked to everyone about what was happening to them in Natal.

The Dutch, who ruled this part of South Africa, were even harsher to the Indians than the English. Gandhi found out who the important people were and tried to meet them. Gandhi shared his dreams. He watched what was going on and thought long and hard about what would help the Indians most. He made a plan.

Gandhi called for a meeting of *all* the Indians living in Pretoria. It didn't matter if they were born in India or their parents were, or even their grandparents. They were all treated the same by the English rulers—even worse by the Dutch. Gandhi was asking all Indians to put aside their differences for once. No one had ever done this. It meant that garbage men, doctors, shopkeepers, gardeners, and even lawyers like Gandhi would sit together.

But word of the young radical had spread in the Indian community. He had written articles for the local Indian newspaper. His ideas were being whispered everywhere. Many, many men came to hear him. They did not bring their wives. It was 1893. Most men felt that women should stay home caring for the house and children. Gandhi looked out as the room filled with Indian men.

He was not nervous at all in front of the crowd. That was a new feeling, but it made sense. He had prepared his speech carefully. But more important than that, this was something he truly believed in.

"My fellow countrymen," he said to get their attention. Then he made a calm list of how unfairly they all were treated. They couldn't own their own land. They couldn't travel first class. "White" hotels and "white" restaurants were off limits to them. They had to stay in their homes after nine o'clock at night. In Pretoria there were streets they could not even walk on. There were many more rules. As Gandhi went on, the crowd began to nod and mutter. They knew all this, but hearing it spelled out made them angry.

Gandhi stopped to let it all sink in. He stood alone on the stage. He was not tall. His voice was quiet, thin, and strangely high-pitched. He was not handsome or famous, but he had everyone's attention. He spoke the truth.

"Part of this is our own fault," he said, then held up his hands for quiet. He explained what he meant. "The whites say we have dirty habits. That *is* true—of some of us. They say we cannot be trusted. Some of us are thieves, yes, and some are sneaky. The whites complain that we can't speak their language. Why, they watch and see that we can't even talk to one another!" Men nodded their heads at this. Many dozens of completely different languages were spoken in India. Indians had brought this confusion of words with them to South Africa. In a way, Gandhi explained, the whites were *right* to think badly of Indians. Before the crowd got angry at this, Gandhi gave them five simple steps to solve the problem.

"First," he said, "*always* tell the truth, even in business." He explained that if every Indian acted honestly, whites would begin to trust "coloreds." They would come to Indian businesses and spend money. The merchants, especially, smiled at this.

"Second," he began. He knew this step would be sensitive. "Adopt more sanitary habits." He suggested that the crowd notice how often whites bathed, how clean they kept their houses, and how tidy their yards were. He pointed out that whites used toilets or dug latrines to get rid of all of their body wastes. "In India, these things do not matter so much," he said. "But the habits of old India makes us look dirty to the English and the Dutch." People shifted in their seats, but they nodded.

"Third," Gandhi said, "learn English." He heard groans. He scolded them, saying that there was no better way to be accepted in white South Africa. "Besides, how could they know how smart we are?" he asked. "They can't understand our jokes, our beautiful poetry, or our clever arguments. They see us making simple hand signs in their businesses, too. We must seem too stupid to learn English. Are we?"

"No!" people said. Some sounded reluctant. Others sounded angry—and proud.

"Fourth," Gandhi went on, "we have to forget all of our caste and religious differences." The crowd was stunned into silence. They had been trained since birth that people were too different to mix. Now this Gandhi fellow was calling for Hindus to work with Muslims—and with Christians, too. He wanted high-caste people to actually work with Untouchables! "This is the only way we can grow strong," Gandhi told them. "Arguing with one another we get nowhere. If we band together we can make a huge difference." People grumbled, but most seemed to see his point.

"And fifth," Gandhi said, "we should form an official association to tell the government what we think about our treatment." He paused to let this sink in. "Together, we do this. Together, we can end the prejudice."

He was done. The hall filled with clapping and stamping feet. Then a crowd of volunteers surged toward the stage. They were ready to form the all-Indian association that Gandhi had suggested.

Calling themselves the Natal Indian Congress, the Indians made a list of things they should do. In the next few weeks they wrote letters to many Dutch government officials. They collected thousands of names of Indians who agreed with them and presented those, too. The Dutch could not ignore this: The Indians were organized, and there were a lot of them. They marched for their rights. That way, the whites could see for themselves how many coloreds there were—and how angry they were about their treatment.

Gandhi used his training to check the legality of everything they did. He also kept writing articles for newspapers. In them he made the same five points he had made in his first speech. He explained his plan again. He wrote about new problems as he heard about them. He gave advice. When writing, he could think through his message and choose his words very carefully. That made his messages even more powerful.

Those newspaper articles were reprinted all over South Africa in Indian newspapers. "Coloreds" talked about them at home and at work. Even Indians who could not read had heard about them. Gandhi's style of writing was to say things simply and in a memorable way. Catchy quotes from his articles spread by word of mouth. Everything he wrote seemed to have a ring of truth to it.

As the months passed, he gathered more and more evidence in Abdullah's case. When they saw the information Gandhi had uncovered, the lawyers for the other side knew they would lose. They decided not to go to court. Instead, in a meeting called "arbitration," they compromised. That way, the problem was solved peacefully. Gandhi liked that. Gandhi had saved the law firms and their clients a great deal of money. They liked that.

His work in Dutch South Africa done, Gandhi could finally go home to India. At last he would see Kasturbai and the little boys.

Back in Durban, where the English ruled, Abdullah insisted on giving Gandhi a farewell party. Gandhi had been good for the business. He had been good for Indians up in Pretoria. His work had given hope to Indians all over South Africa. Many of Abdullah's important business friends came to the all-day party.

After lunch, Gandhi stepped out. He needed some fresh air. He wanted a last look at South Africa before he left. As he walked along a street, an English newspaper headline caught his eye: INDIAN FRANCHISE! Gandhi stopped. He read the article there in the street. The British were trying to pass a law that said no Indians could vote!

Gandhi was furious. Indians were citizens of the British Commonwealth. How could they lose the right to vote in English South Africa?

He bought the newspaper and stormed back to his party. "Did you see this?" he demanded.

"No, I only read the Indian papers," Abdullah said. His friends agreed. Gandhi explained the article to them. Some Englishmen were arguing that Indians were too simple to understand what voting means. The vote seemed sure to pass.

"If we lose the vote here, we will have no way to block laws written against us. We could not elect officials who are fair to Indians. Conditions here would be as bad as they are in Dutch South Africa!" That got the Indian's attention.

"What can we do?" they cried.

"I have some ideas," Gandhi began. Abdullah's friends listened and agreed.

"You must stay and help us fight this!" they argued. In the end, Gandhi agreed to stay in South Africa for an extra month. He wrote articles for Indian and English papers. He gave speeches and wrote letters.

It was too late.

The dreadful law passed. Now Indians could not vote. Gandhi agreed to stay a few months longer while he created a petition that Indians all through the country could sign. It would be sent to Queen Victoria's colonial secretary in London. Ten thousand Indians signed the protest letter. Again, Gandhi prepared to go home.

"Stay on!" Abdullah's friends urged Gandhi after three months. "We will give you all the business you need to live well here as a lawyer. Indians here need you!" Gandhi agreed. Abdullah found a house for him in Durban. Gandhi appeared before the Supreme Court arguing that he be allowed to practice law. It took months, but he got permission. Gandhi became the first colored lawyer in South Africa. Abdullah's friends gave him all the legal work he could handle over the next two years. Other businesses hired him. He became wealthy.

His house filled up quickly. His law clerks and his secretaries lived there with their families. Other Indians who were fighting for equality came by to talk. Groups met in his living room. Travelers from the Dutch areas of South Africa stayed, learned, and took Gandhi's ideas back with them. He founded the Natal Indian Congress, a resistance group dedicated to eliminating prejudice against "browns." They organized work stoppages. That made the employers see how important Indians were to their businesses. Gandhi kept writing letters, pamphlets, and newspaper articles. They were published all over South Africa but also in India and in England, too.

At the end of three years, Gandhi told his friends that he had to bring his wife and children to live with him. He went back to India in 1896 for six months to close out his life there. But Gandhi had changed. He was too full of his life's passion to relax. In India, he gave speeches and wrote more articles about the conditions in Africa. He met with important political leaders. They were glad to get to know this famous young man. Gandhi learned from them. Gokhale Krishna, especially, taught Gandhi valuable lessons about how to get power in a government—and then how to use it. The men became friends.

When Gandhi's boat returned to Durban in South Africa, the authorities refused to let him get off. The ship waited at anchor for three weeks. When he finally was released, a mob of whites had gathered at the docks. They were angry that Gandhi was getting more rights for the coloreds. They felt they were losing their power. They beat him up as he walked off the ship.

The police protected him. Kasturbai, now pregnant again, Harilal, and Manilal got off safely too. Gandhi told everyone that he was not upset.

The people in England were furious when they heard about it. The famous Gandhi, beaten by a crowd of Englishmen? Gandhi's fans in England made such a fuss that their government said his attackers should be sent to jail.

Gandhi said no.

Around the world, people heard about this kind, gentle Indian who did not want justice for himself. He only wanted justice for his countrymen. The South African government, embarrassed by all the publicity, reversed itself. They gave all Indians back their right to vote.

Gandhi had won—but there was more to do. As always, he had been thinking. Well-to-do Indians were used to relying on others to live. They had cooks, gardeners, and house-maids. They had Untouchables for the dirtiest tasks. And even the Untouchables had to rely on farmers to grow their food and sellers at the marketplace to get it to them. No wonder Indians carried a prejudice against themselves, Gandhi thought. Without all these helpers, they could not survive.

If we could become *self*-reliant, Gandhi reasoned, we would have more pride. With more self-esteem, Indians could fight wholeheartedly against prejudice.

But Gandhi didn't just come up with ideas. He lived them. "In this house," he told his startled family, his law clerks, and his secretaries, "we are all equals. Everyone will take a turn at cooking. Everyone will sweep the floors. Everyone will clean out the chamber pots." That made everyone gasp.

There were no toilets in the house in Durban. This was true of most of the world at that time. When people had to go to the bathroom, they squatted over a wide pot that was usually hidden under a bed or covered with a pretty lid. Someone had to carry these posts outside and empty them every day. Then they had to be washed. It was the worst household chore.

"You cannot mean that!" Kasturbai said angrily. "I am a Vaishya, wife of the famous and rich Mohandas K. Gandhi! I do *not* do the chores of an Untouchable!"

Gandhi had been writing about how

Indians were too prejudiced to fight prejudice in South Africa. They all grew up treating Untouchables worse than whites ever treated coloreds or even blacks. It was just as bad, Gandhi wrote, that Untouchables grew up expecting this treatment.

But Kasturbai still could not read. She had read nothing of the thousands of words her husband had written explaining his startling philosophy.

They stared at each other. "You *will* take a turn at every chore here," Gandhi said. He tried to explain. They argued for hours. In the end, he insisted. "You are my wife. You will wash the chamber pots, like all the rest of us."

Word of this strange house of equality spread along with Gandhi's idea of self-reliance. Gandhi even studied medicine so his house would not have to rely on a doctor's help. He helped Kasturbai deliver his third child. They named the healthy little boy Ramdas. Another boy came a few years later. He was called Devdas. The boys were ready for school, but Gandhi did not want to rely on schoolteachers. "You will teach them at home," he told his wife. "I want them to know the language and religion of our families."

In 1899, the Dutch and English began a war over control of South Africa. Coloreds were not allowed to fight, even though they were voting citizens of the British Commonwealth. Gandhi was furious. "This is just another case of English prejudice!" he argued. He did not want to go to battle. That went against his vow of nonviolence, ahisma. But Mother England needed him! Gandhi organized Indian ambulance crews. He called for hundreds of men to volunteer to carry wounded soldiers away on stretchers.

"Why should we?" they asked. He told them that the English would remember their service. That they would forever think of Indians differently. That it would help fight prejudice. The English army still refused to let "coloreds" serve. But when the war went badly, they finally asked Gandhi's men to help. He sent the Indians to the battle grounds. He left home to lead an ambulance crew.

The English won the war against the Dutch, called the Boer War. And they gave Gandhi a medal for his service, his courage and his help.

But there were more troubles brewing for the Indians in South Africa. Gandhi knew he would be staying. He bought a ninety-acre farm near Durban. He called it Phoenix Settlement, after a little town nearby. He had long thought that self-reliant Indians should grow their own food. Now his thinking turned deeper. He wanted to give up money and belongings and spend his life doing good. To him this meant developing his philosophy.

Gandhi moved a weekly newspaper to the farm, too. The *Indian Opinion* had been publishing for years. It printed copies in English and three different Indian languages. It was perfect for spreading his ideas. Now he wrote self-help articles about farming and clean water, nonviolence, and medicine—anything that would help Indians become self-reliant.

In 1906, he formed another ambulance crew to help in another English war. This time they were fighting native blacks from the Zulu tribe. During the war, Gandhi had another breakthrough in thought. He decided to devote his future to public service. He remembered the *Brahmacharya,* an ancient Hindu vow taken by holy men to develop their inner strength. No more anger or arguments, he told himself, no more feasting, no more good clothes or new belongings, and no more intimacy with women. He would have to always remain calm. Just the thought of trying for this level of perfection thrilled him.

Now when he returned to Phoenix Settlement, people called it an *ashram* because it was led by a holy man—Mohandas K. Gandhi. He preached the doctrine of *Satyagraha.* That meant staying firm and honest and loving in the fight for a good cause. He wrote about Satyagraha in the newspaper, gave speeches about it, and lived it.

A test came when the government insisted that every Indian and black in South Africa be fingerprinted and given a photo ID. They had to carry this card everywhere. "We are not common criminals," Gandhi said calmly. "We must refuse." At a huge rally in 1908, Gandhi led the way by burning his card. Others followed—and then they all sang the British national anthem, "God Save the Queen." That reminded everyone that they were still loyal British citizens. They were just refusing to obey this law.

When he was arrested he told the judge to send him to jail. It was absurd. That was the point. By refusing to follow the rules, Gandhi showed how silly they were. Gandhi went to jail and spent the time reading and thinking. Soon, thousands of his followers crowded the jails. As soon as they were let out, they broke the card-carrying rule and got themselves re-arrested. Soon the jails could hold no more. By 1909, Gandhi was called to London to talk with authorities there. For months he argued his cause. The English would not budge.

On the way home to Phoenix Settlement, Gandhi wrote a new essay. For a change, it didn't deal with South Africa. Instead, he carefully made the case for India itself to split from England. He titled it "Indian Home Rule."

A British colony declaring independence from Mother England? That hadn't happened since America broke away in 1776. It was a revolutionary idea.

There was more conflict in South Africa over the next years. Gandhi was always at the front of the nonviolent fight, speaking softly and practicing Satyagraha. He was jailed again and again. He founded other ashrams in the country and wrote hundreds and hundreds of articles. In the end, laws were changed. Around the world people followed his struggles—and his successes.

At forty-one, Gandhi could return to India at last.

# CHAPTER 9

# TAKING THE FIGHT HOME

Gokhale, Gandhi's wise old friend, was dying. He asked Gandhi one last favor. "Promise me that you'll spend one full year in silence," he asked. "Before you start pushing Indians to fight for justice, you need to know them better. You need to know India." Gandhi was eager to get to work, but he saw his friend's point.

He'd been gone for more than twenty years. Groups of Indian revolutionaries were already calling on him to take the lead. They wanted freedom from English rule. They knew what Gandhi had done in South Africa. "What should we do next?" they asked the famous man. Gandhi did not know what actions to suggest to them or where.

He took the trip Gokhale suggested. The size of India was far greater than he had remembered. So were the poverty, filth, disease, and hopelessness of many Indian's lives. From railroad cars, he saw craggy, snowcapped mountains. Light green rice paddies whisked by the windows. Magnificent old temples. Filthy cities crowded with life. Beautiful beaches and deep forests. This was all his country. Gandhi took it all in and thought.

He did not want India to fight a bloody revolution. Hundreds of thousands of the people he saw would die. The cities and roads and bridges would be bombed. Those precious ancient buildings would be destroyed. Gandhi knew he had to lead a nonviolent revolution. First, he needed to show Indians how Satyagraha worked in action.

When Gandhi was ready to settle down, people were happy to donate to this holy man.

With their funding, Gandhi founded a new ashram where he could study, think, and write. He called it Satyagraha Ashram, to spread the name of his philosophy. This one would be based on weaving, with everyone making fabric for their own clothing and to sell. Twenty people from Phoenix Settlement came with him. Gandhi's two older boys had left home by now, but there were new followers.

This time Gandhi insisted that they include a family of Untouchables. "No!" Kasturbai said. "I will not live in the same home with Untouchables—even for you."

"No!" said the donors who had promised money to the new ashram.

"No!" said the local clothing companies. They had agreed to buy cloth from the new ashram. "If your workers mix with Untouchables, we won't buy from you."

Gandhi insisted. The new low-caste family moved in. At first no one but Gandhi would speak to them. The ashram nearly went broke—until someone secretly handed Gandhi enough money to last a full year.

Kasturbai agreed to stay. Gandhi had included her in some of his protests in India. She had given speeches. She had even led marches of women. Her husband had given her opportunities no other Indian woman had ever enjoyed before. He would bring the voices of women into India's revolution.

A message one day told Gandhi where to start his fight. "Help us!" an indigo farmer pleaded. "A new blue dye has been invented. No one is buying our indigo now. We are out of work. We are starving. But our landlords are demanding rent—in cash. Thousands will soon be homeless."

Gandhi hurried back to the far north of India. He was arrested as a troublemaker. Once free again he helped rewrite the agreements so farmers got a payment for work they had done. They were allowed to stay on their land. A year later he returned again. Ten thousand factory workers in the north were employed making cloth. Gandhi knew the factory owners. They paid workers such low wages that the workers went hungry. They could not buy food for their families.

Gandhi and the owners met. He demanded a raise for the workers. The answer was no. Gandhi urged the workers to go on strike. Without workers the factories could not make cloth. They shut down. Every day, Gandhi met with groups of striking workers. He pleaded with them to stay off the job. Sooner or later, he told them, the factory owners would give in.

When the workers began to give up, Gandhi had an idea. He spoke with them. He spoke with the owners, too. "I am not going to eat until you both agree to bargain," he said. All over India, people read that the holy man Gandhi was putting his life on the line for the workers. Nothing happened on the first day. Nothing happened on the second, either. Gandhi kept writing, of course. The more people who read about this, the better.

At the end of the third day the factory owners gave in. Talks began, and the workers were given "a living wage." Now they had enough to feed themselves and their families.

And now Gandhi had a new nonviolent weapon. People everywhere cared about him. They all called him "Bapu" as if he were their wise old father. They called him *Mahatma* Gandhi, meaning "great soul." They cared about his health. They would do anything to keep their "Bapu" from starving himself to death.

It was 1919 now. World War 1 was over. All of India waited for England to keep its promises. Gandhi, with other Indians, had formed ambulance crews. They worked alongside the British soldiers in the war. As thanks, England had promised to give them more freedom in their homeland.

Instead, they were making things harder.

They made harsh laws and increased taxes. Gandhi led protests on paper, sending letters and petitions to the government. He also led rallies. He told all Indians to burn the medals they had been given for service in the war. Photographers and newsmen from around the world covered this protest. They reported that the protestors sang "God Save the Queen," too.

Gandhi was invited to a top meeting of Muslim leaders from all over the Middle East. They needed his help, too. The English, working with the Americans and Russians, had made a terrible mistake. At the very end of the war, they'd changed the map of the Middle East. They drew new borders so that Islam's two most holy cities, Mecca and Medina, were in different countries. The Muslim businessmen in South Africa had helped Gandhi. Now, they thought, he should use his fame and political strength to help their cause.

This was not Gandhi's fight. He had sworn to get justice for Indians from England. He felt he couldn't take on the big Muslim problem, too. Instead, he told these leaders to tell the Muslims to work together with Hindus in India. The leaders were angry with him. Gandhi had made powerful enemies, though he did not seem to know it.

He did know his next step at home. He had been wearing fancy suits made in England for years. Now he learned how to spin cotton thread from the fluffy seed bolls made by cotton plants. He used a small, old-fashioned spinning wheel. He taught spinning to everyone in his ashram. They wove a thick white cloth called *khadi* from the thread they had made. Gandhi dressed in shirts and pants of khadi. That way he did not have to rely on clothing made in England.

Then Gandhi called rallies in many towns. He arrived at each one dressed in clothing that he had made for himself. He talked about self-reliance. He explained what he had done. "If we all make our own clothes," he said, "we can prove we don't need England. We can stop sending them our money, too. Who will join me?" he challenged in his thin, high voice. "Who will burn their English-made clothes and rely on yourselves for a change?"

One by one, men pulled off their jackets. They took off fancy shirts and bow ties. They took off socks and shoes. They threw everything into a huge pile. Gandhi struck the match. The piles burned for days. In a few months everyone seemed to be wearing khadi. It became the style—a patriotic fashion.

Even seeing the Indian patriots all around them, the English didn't seem to take them seriously. Gandhi called for all workers everywhere in the country to strike. "Stay home for one day," he told everyone. "Spend the time praying and fasting and thinking about how badly we are treated by England." On that day the English had no one to weed their gardens; no one to care for their children, clean their clothes, or serve them tea. They were a little frightened. Mostly they were angry.

So were the Indians. In some places they forgot Satyagraha. They fought with police and injured some Englishmen and their families. There was rioting in some cities, especially Amritsar. It made Gandhi sick. What had happened to ahisma? Under Satyagraha, no one was supposed to be hurt! He called off the strike. "Go back to work!" he ordered.

One English military officer in Amritsar was so angry, he ordered his troops to shoot a huge crowd of peaceful protestors dead. Three hundred and seventy-nine babies, women, children, men, and grandparents were killed. One thousand and two hundred more Indians were left wounded. Not a single one of them had carried a gun.

It made the news world-wide. The Amritsar massacre changed Gandhi's faith in the goodness of the English law. Before, he'd fought for justice under the English rule. Now he would fight to make India a free country. But he would do it peacefully.

Gandhi traveled all over India for months.

Vast crowds gathered to see the Mahatma. When he spoke now he insisted on non-violence. Gandhi knew that the poorest of the people he was speaking to could not afford to throw all their clothes into a fire. To show them how cheaply they could dress, he showed them. He stopped wearing sewn shirts or trousers. He gave up his cap, even though, at forty-five, he was bald. Instead, he wound a length of khadi cloth around and between his legs. This loincloth, called a dhoti, hung down almost to his knees. He gave up shoes, too. He protected his feet in homemade sandals. Copying him, even the poorest Indian could fight for independence.

A new English viceroy came to take charge of India. He wanted to throw Gandhi in jail. But Gandhi hadn't actually broken any laws.

He called for another rally in the big city of Bombay. It would be completely peaceful. Thousands of supporters showed up. The English wanted to break up the protest, but this time, Satyagraha worked the way it should. There was nothing to arrest the khaki-wearing Indians for. They could not be shot. There was nothing the frustrated English could do.

In the other side of town, criminals began attacking visitors from the royal court in England. They wore dhotis and said they were Gandhi's fighters. There were clashes between police and these fake patriots.

Gandhi knew he had stirred up all the unrest in India. The deaths were his fault. He fasted for five days to cleanse himself. He vowed to spend every Monday in silence and prayer.

He was arrested soon after that. "You are charged with sedition," the English judge told him. "You have urged people to fight against England." The world press reported a speech Gandhi was said to have made in this "Great Trial." He said he was guilty. He explained why he wanted Indian independence. England was using its power and laws to harm Indians. And he said the judge would be wrong if he didn't send him to jail.

There was nothing else the judge could do. He sentenced Mahatmas Gandhi, holy man and beloved Bapu to millions of Indians, to jail for six years.

Gandhi spent his time in jail as a spiritual retreat. He prayed. He read and studied great books. He spun his spinning wheel constantly. And he wrote. India, and the world, read Gandhi's newspaper articles. People learned new ways to be self-reliant. They studied his essays on philosophy. Famous people got letters from him, and wrote back. Mahatma was captive—but he was not silent.

# CHAPTER 10
# THE SALT MARCH

In 1924, Mahatma Gandhi was released early from prison. He had only served two years. His health was not good, and the English were afraid he would die in jail. Then all Indians would rise up in anger.

He had written a book, *The History of Satyagraha in South Africa* in jail. He had begun to write *The Story of My Experiments with the Truth,* too. He had stayed in touch with all of his friends at the Indian National Congress. That was the huge organization that had grown up to support Gandhi's drives for independence.

But things had changed. While Gandhi was in prison the Hindus had become more and more upset because the Muslims were killing cows. The Muslims hated how Hindus kept making noise during their five daily prayer periods. The two groups had drawn apart. The Indian National Congress had broken in two. Hindus stayed, but the Muslims made their own organization, the Muslim League.

Nothing Gandhi wrote in his newspaper or said in speeches seemed to help. The hatred and anger grew. Finally riots broke out. Muslims and Hindus killed each other—though they once fought the Raj together. Gandhi was horrified.

"I will eat nothing for three weeks," he told the world. "I drink only water with a little salt. I do this as a prayer for peace—and as a penance for getting everyone stirred up in the first place. At the end I will meet with leaders from both religions plus the English." That got people's attention. Gandhi was still their Bapu. Thousands of people rushed to see him wherever he went. They bowed to the ground in front of him. They kissed his hands and feet. And now, every time they ate for the next twenty-one days they would have to think of Mahatma's growing hunger. They would remember that he was fasting because of the hatred they had let grow in their hearts.

And he chose to fast in the house of a Muslim friend. He had Muslim doctors to watch over him. This sent a powerful message to the Hindus: Gandhi would trust the Muslims with his life.

Within a week, meetings between religious leaders were held. They agreed to cooperate. They even ate together to prove their new friendship. "But I promised to fast for three weeks," Gandhi said when they told him he could eat again.

He grew weaker and weaker. Finally he could not even walk. He lay on a bed. Would he die before the twenty-first day was over? The whole nation held its breath. On the last morning, leaders gathered by his bedside. Christians sang a hymn. Muslims read from the Koran. Hindus said verses from the *Bhagavad Gita*. They promised to work together.

A friend held Gandhi's head up. He brought a saucer of orange juice to Gandhi's lips. At long, long last, the Mahatma swallowed. His fast was over! And it had succeeded.

Gandhi had not served all the jail time he'd thought he should under the law. For the rest of his six-year sentence he gave speeches and held rallies, wrote for newspapers, and gave interviews about his philosophy.

He gave people a simple way to remember how to practice Satyagraha. He would hold up one finger and say, "This is for equality for Untouchables. The next finger is for spinning." He held up a third finger. "This is for avoiding alcohol and drugs. The fourth is for Hindu-Muslim friendship. The fifth, for equality for women." Then he pointed to the wrist that connected them all: "This is nonviolence."

In December of 1928, the Indian National Congress gave the Raj a deadline. By the end of the year, they wanted self-rule. The deadline passed. Nothing changed. Now Gandhi took up the fight for independence—but in a strange, nonviolent way.

He knew that humans needed salt to live. The English knew this too. They controlled all the salt mining in India. They made it against the law to get your own salt. That way, the Raj kept every single Indian dependent on them for survival. The Mahatma announced that he was going to lead a march to the sea to gather his own salt. "Everyone is welcome to join me."

The sixty-one-year-old Bapu left from his ashram with a few friends. Reporters and cameramen followed them. The road along his two-hundred-mile walk was lined by supporters dressed in khadi. They cheered loudly as he approached. Then they knelt as he passed. Gandhi stopped at every village. "When I give the sign," he told them, "everyone should start making salt for themselves. You will be breaking the law. You might have to pay a fine. You might even go to jail."

He knew that he might be arrested. On the twenty-fourth day of the march, Gandhi stooped at the edge of the ocean. He held up a pinch of salt. "Now," he said. The word spread like wildfire. From one end of India to the other, everyone broke the law.

There was no way to arrest the whole country. Again, Gandhi had made the Raj look helpless against the huge mass of Indians yearning to be free. They arrested the Mahatma. Then they arrested his sons and a few other people behind them. All the while the cameras were rolling. By now, thousands of people had joined the march to the sea. The English gave up and the beach filled with Indians breaking the law for a few grains of salt.

Gandhi was thrown in jail again. This time there was no trial. The authorities did not want to give Gandhi another chance to make a speech against them.

That only increased the protests. All over India, people were breaking laws. One hundred thousand were arrested. The police, frantic that they were losing control, began beating people. The army joined in. The Raj allowed this. They did not want to lose India.

But the world was watching the brutality. Even the government in England grew ashamed. At last they decided to release Gandhi. In 1931, the viceroy of India invited Gandhi to his beautiful palace. Wearing sandals, his dhoti, and a shawl for warmth, the Mahatma sat down to bargain. "All Indians may make salt for themselves," the Raj announced. At last the English were talking *with* the Indians instead of just making rules for them. Gandhi was happy—but he had more to do.

He founded a new ashram in the country far, far from any trains or main roads. Still, people traveled to meet him. Indians felt that just seeing their Bapu would give them a blessing. Newspaper reporters knew he was making history. Religious scholars wanted to discuss philosophy with him. The new head of the Indian National Congress, Jawaharlal Nehru, came to talk. A young woman from England arrived too. Mirabehn went right to work, practicing Satyagraha. Kasturbai and Gandhi welcomed her help. England entered World War II and decided that India must fight. The Indians refused. Battles raged around them. They fought battles at home too. The Raj hadn't given up.

They shut the Indian National Congress down and took all of its money. They closed down Gandhi's newspaper. They put him in jail again for plotting against their government. They arrested more than thirty-two thousand political prisoners across the country.

But the whites knew that they were vastly outnumbered in India. They felt if they could split up the country again, they could get control back. They announced that the Muslims would have their own government. They could elect their own representatives. There would be a separate organization for Hindus. The

Untouchables would have a whole other set of officials. And all three would still be under the rule of the English.

Gandhi had worked for forty years to bring people of every caste together. Now the British were tearing them apart. He started another fast. "I will starve myself to death this time," he said, "if this terrible plan is not stopped."

All of India worked to save his life. Untouchables were allowed into temples for the first time in centuries. They were allowed to get water from public wells. Hindus and Muslims invited them to dinner. Leaders held emergency meetings.

Bapu was old. He was weak. The jail sent for Kasturbai. "Can you help him?" the authorities pleaded. She rubbed his arms as he lay weakly in his bed. She made him drink some water. Still, on the fourth day, doctors said his condition was critical.

The Indians agreed to unite again. "Tell Gandhi to eat!"

The holy man lay dying. "No," he said. "I

will break fast only when the prime minister in London approves this agreement." It was the weekend in England, but a messenger hurried to the prime minister's home. He signed the Yeravda Pact. Gandhi—and Indian unity—was saved.

# CHAPTER 11

# "QUIT INDIA!"

On August 8, 1942, the Indian National Conference met and passed a resolution calling for England to "Quit India." "British rule must end immediately," they said. If it didn't, Gandhi, the Blessed One, would launch a total resistance campaign. The leaders wrote up a constitution for their new country.

Gandhi went to see the viceroy that very evening to plead that he accept the document. He knew what might happen if the Indians were disappointed again.

Overnight, Gandhi and Kasturbai and Nehru and other leaders were imprisoned. The jails were full, so they got to stay under guard in an actual palace. It might have been beautiful, but it had become a prison.

Indians rioted. How dare the viceroy arrest all those good people? It only proved that the English were out to crush India—and Indians. Crowds attacked members of the Raj, their guards, and policemen. They burned official buildings and cut telegraph lines. Protestors blocked roads and ruined railroad tracks.

The viceroy said it was Gandhi's fault. Gandhi argued that the viceroy had brought this on himself. Then Gandhi fasted for three weeks in protest. It made the Indians even angrier that their beloved Bapu had to suffer again. They kept fighting.

After a few weeks, Gandhi's secretary died. He had become a close family friend. His death threw Kasturbai into a depression.

Two years later, she died in jail. Gandhi had been married to her for sixty-two years—since he was a child.

The shock of it weakened him, and he fell ill too. The Raj did not want him to die in jail. That would make the people even angrier.

They released him. Gandhi was seventy-five but he was not about to retire.

There was more trouble. Jinnah, the leader of the Muslims, was making new demands. "We cannot live in an India full of Hindus!" he told screaming crowds of Muslims. "We need our own country—a Muslim-only country."

Two Indias? "I would sooner cut myself in half," Gandhi said when he heard.

But Jinnah and his people were serious. "We will not cooperate with you," he said.

World War II was over in 1945. England turned her attention to the India problem. It took a year, but they promised India freedom from all British rule. A new viceroy, Lord Louis Mountbatten, a member of the royal family, came to help with the changeover. Indians were named to all the official positions. Jawaharlal Nehru became prime minister.

Jinnah was furious that he had not been chosen instead. He called for a Muslim day of "Direct

Action." On August 16, 1946, they began four days of bloody rioting. Five thousand people were killed. Fifteen thousand were injured. The victims were mostly Muslims. This religious civil war spread around the country. Gandhi traveled everywhere, pleading for calm.

His visits stopped the fighting—but only for a while. Lord Mountbatten sent for Nehru and Jinnah to come to his office and settle things. He asked Mahatma Gandhi to come and help. Nothing Gandhi, the viceroy, or Nehru said could convince Jinnah that his Muslim people would be safe in a mixed India.

Mountbatten made a new map. It carved out a Muslim country on each side of India. He named it Pakistan. There were many Hindus living in this new country. There were many Muslims left in India. A period of sorrow and violence followed. People left their family homes and moved to where their religion fit. Not everyone was willing to move. Those who wouldn't go were sometimes attacked. Fights broke out. People died.

On August 15, 1947, India became independent. The rioting went on and on in the huge city of Calcutta. Gandhi went there to see what he could do. He was nearly beaten by a mob, so he left for Delhi. There was rioting there too: Hindu against Muslim.

Gandhi tried to quiet the situation. Nothing he did worked. He decided to fast to death again if the fighting didn't stop. The Indian government paid the Pakistani government money it had owed since the new maps were drawn. A hundred important men signed a pledge of peace and brotherhood and brought it to Gandhi.

He finally ate something, but he was terribly weak. He was also seventy-eight. On January 30, 1948, Gandhi asked for helpers to help him walk to a prayer meeting. Leaning each arm on a young woman, Gandhi began the short walk to a platform. Five hundred people crowded around to hear the wisdom of their master.

Suddenly a Muslim man bowed to Gandhi. He reached into his jacket. He pulled out a gun and fired at the Mahatma. As he felt three bullets enter his body, Gandhi cried out, "Oh, God. *Hey, Ram!*" He died in prayer to his God.

The whole world mourned the passing of this truly great and holy man. Christians everywhere knew of the Indian patriot who had always turned the other cheek. Hindus had come to worship him. Muslims knew he had fought for their rights, too. Everyone, it seemed, had been touched by his teaching. They had read his wise sayings and his writings, or had heard his speeches on the radio.

Even today, and far from India, the name Gandhi is well known. People still read his books. Many still try to live Satyagraha, fighting wrongs through nonviolence. The Mahatma's quotes are printed on greeting cards, mugs, and calendars. They bring inspiration to anyone who reads them.

# GANDHI'S FAMOUS SAYINGS

Many of Mahatma Gandhi's words have become famous for their wisdom.

Here is a small sample:

*Be the change you want to see in the world.*

*An eye for an eye makes the whole world blind.*

*Happiness is when what you think, what you say, and what you do are in harmony.*

*Freedom is not worth having if it does not include the freedom to make mistakes.*

*I am prepared to die, but there is no cause for which I am prepared to kill.*

*Strength does not come from physical capacity. It comes from an indomitable will.*

*There is more to life than simply increasing its speed.*

*They cannot take away our self-respect if we do not give it to them.*

*Live as if you were to die tomorrow.*

*The weak can never forgive. Forgiveness is an attribute of the strong.*

*You must not lose your faith in humanity. Humanity is an ocean. If a few drops of the ocean are dirty, the ocean does not become dirty.*

*If we wish to create a lasting peace, we must begin with the children.*

# GLOSSARY OF INDIAN WORDS

Ahisma: ancient Hindu teaching of non-violence

ashram: a religious community

ba: the Indian word for "mother"

bapu: the Indian word for "father"

*Bhagavad Gita*: one of the Hindu holy texts written as a 700-stanza poem

Brahmin: the top caste in India; scholars and priests

chatmuras: the rainy season in India; five months, starting around December

Dharma: duty; what you should do in your job, your religion, your life dhoti: a loincloth wrapping woven and worn by the poorest Indians

Hinduism: the oldest religion still practiced on Earth today

Karma: the result of your actions, good or bad, in your soul and your life

khadi: a rough cotton cloth woven by hand

Namaste: Indian greeting of deep respect

Satyagraha: nonviolent, calm, and loving resistance to injustice

Vaisya: the third Indian caste; merchants, skilled workers, and farmers

# TIME LINE OF GANDHI'S LIFE

1869 Mohandas K. Gandhi born October 2, in Porbandar, western India

1882 Gandhi marries Kasturbai Nakanji. Both are thirteen years old

1888 Gandhi goes to England to study law

1893 Gandhi goes to South Africa to practice law; decides to fight prejudice

1908 Gandhi gives up law practice to fight for Indian equality

1910 Gandhi starts his first ashram, Tolstoy Farm, in South Africa

1914 Gandhi returns to India, travels, and opens another ashram

1920 Gandhi writes constitution for Indian National Congress; is called "Mahatma"

1922 Gandhi is arrested; makes statement at his "Great Trial" and is sent to jail

1929 Gandhi leads the salt march and is sent to jail again

1932 Gandhi fasts until the Yeravda Pact is signed

1942 The Indian National Congress says, "Quit India." Gandhi is jailed

1944 Kasturbai dies on February 22. On May 6, Gandhi is let out of prison for the final time

1946 England promises to free India, but Muslims demand a separate country

1947 India and Pakistan become independent
of England on August 15

1948 Gandhi, seventy-eight, is assassinated on
his way to a prayer meeting on January 30

# FOR MORE
# INFORMATION

## PICTURE BOOK

Demi, *Gandhi*, Margaret McElderry Books,
NY, 2001.

## MIDDLE GRADE BOOKS

Cheney, Glenn Alan, *Mohandus Gandhi*,
Franklin Watts, NY, 1983.

Montgomery, Elizabeth Rider, *Peaceful Fighter,
Gandhi*, Garrard Publishing, Champaign,
IL, 1970.

Severance, John B., *Gandhi, Great Soul*,
Clarion Books, NY, 1997.

# FOR ADULTS

Gandhi, Mohandus K. *Gandhi, An Autobiography; The Story of My Experiments with Truth*, Beacon Press, Boston, 1957.

# VIDEOS

*Gandhi,* Carolina Bank, Ltd. and National Film Development Corp. Ltd., 1982; Columbia TriStar Home Entertainment, 2001.

# WEBSITES

www.brainyquote.com/quotes/author/m/mohandas_gandhi.html
Brainy Quotes, *Brainy Quotes by Mohandus Gandhi.*
Gandhi's best-loved quotes—and some very surprising ones.

www.bbc.o.uk/history/historic_figures/gandhi_
mohandus.shtml
British Broadcasting Company, *Mohandas
Gandhi(1869-1948)*.
Great facts and links at this site plus a
recording of Gandhi's voice.

www.mahatma.org.in/
Mahatma Gandhi Foundation, *The Official
Mahatma Gandhi e-Archive and Reference
Library*.
Many photographs and documents.

www.time.com/time/time100/leaders/profile/
gandhi.html
*Time* magazine, "Time 100: Mohandas
Gandhi."
*Time* magazine's reasons for listing Gandhi
as one of the top 100 leaders of the last
century.